What People are Saying about THREADS

This is the book I've been urging Ron to write for the last ten years. I have been in the ministry for over thirty years, and Ron is one of the most radical yet practical Christians I have ever known. His incredible devotion to the Lord and the gospel has given him a voice that is more than worthy of your time and attention. The threads he speaks of are deeply woven into his own life and will give you wisdom and direction for your journey!

-Jeff King, President, International Christian Concern

THREADS is written by someone who knows what he's talking about. For the 20-plus years I have known Ron, I've watched him use his uncanny ability to help people step into their best life—one that is personally fulfilling and pleasing to God. That's what he does in this book. He leans into Biblical truth and his own experience to enrich our understanding of God in a way that transforms how we think and live."

-Ray Holden, President & COO, Millers Ale House

Occasionally a book comes across my desk that is unique and filled with both practical and biblical wisdom. THREADS is one of those books. It is a beautiful weaving of the lessons Ron has learned in life that is masterfully tied to God's Word to create 10 Iron Sharpens Iron takeaways. This is a must-read with timely and relevant pearls of wisdom for every person, regardless of where they are on their spiritual journey.

-David Hill, Founder, IronMen of God

There has never been a more crucial time in society when we've needed a book like THREADS. I've known Ron Tewson for over a decade and watched as he's dedicated his life to not only help us understand the wonder of God, but to inject His priceless teachings into our everyday lives. THREADS does this in a relatable and digestible way and will leave you in a far better place mentally and spiritually than before you opened the book.

-Martin Khodabakhshian, 15-Time Emmy Winning Director/Producer, ESPN

THREADS

All Scripture quotations, unless otherwise noted, are taken from the *New American Standard Bible* (NASB), copyright 1960, 1962, 1963, 1968, 1971, 1972, 1973, 1975, 1977, 1995, by The Lockman Foundation. Used by permission. www.Lockman.org.

Scripture quotations notated NIV are taken from the *Holy Bible, New International Version* NIV. Copyright 1973, 1978, 1984, 2011 by Biblica Inc. Used by permission. All rights reserved worldwide.

Scripture quotations notated NLT are taken from the *Holy Bible, New Living Translation* copyright 1996, 2004, 2007. Used by permission of Tyndale House Publishers, Inc., Carol Stream, IL 60188. All rights reserved.

Bold in Scripture quotations has been added by the author for emphasis.

ISBN Print edition: 979-8-9868443-0-5
ISBN E-book edition: 979-8-9868443-1-2
Library of Congress Control Number: 2022915976

Cover design and layout by Scott Wolf

Published in the United States of America.
First Edition, 2022

THREADS

Weaving a Life of
Peace & Purpose
in a Chaotic World

CONTENTS

Introduction

READ THIS FIRST!

I'm a follower of Jesus Christ. I don't mean I simply believe that Jesus was a good person who taught some great things and is one of the leading religious figures of history. All this is true, yet it's much more.

I was born in America, and Christianity was part of my heritage. I grew up in a good church with good people who had a positive influence on me. But as I got older and began traveling to parts of the world where people believed differently, I had to make some decisions. And I did. That is why today I have much more than a belief: I have a relationship with the infinite-personal God that affects my thinking, choices, actions, and entire life. Without apology, I'm a follower and friend of Jesus.

A couple of years ago I did a search to see the topics Christian publishers were most interested in publishing. It was during the Covid 19 pandemic, and many had to do with wading through the deep waters of anxiety, stress, fear, loss, and uncertainty. I then looked to see the subjects most commonly being preached from our church's pulpits, and it was much the same.

I found this pretty disheartening. I can understand it being true of those who have no hope beyond themselves, but NOT for ones claiming to have a relationship with the living God.

And then it hit me. Somewhere along the way, too many had failed to weave the threads of the fullness of God into the fabric of their everyday lives. Somewhere along the way, too many were unable to connect the unchanging realities of God to the ever-changing chaos of our world. And somewhere along the way, too many had lost the ability to live in the confidence of the Old Testament prophet:

> *Even though the fig trees have no blossoms, and there are no grapes on the vines; even though the olive crop fails, and the fields lie empty and barren; even though the flocks die in the fields, and the cattle barns are empty, yet I will rejoice in the LORD! I will be joyful in the God of my salvation! The Sovereign LORD is my strength! He makes me as surefooted as a deer, able to tread upon the heights.*
> Habakkuk 3:17-19 NLT

Each of us lives with seen and unseen realities, yet it's the threads of the unseen that create the narrative that writes our story. While they may not be visible like birds or clouds, we know they exist because of their effects. And the quality of the invisible threads we choose will determine how well we navigate the chaos of our world.

Some of you have chosen the wrong threads and they're unraveling. Life's circumstances have left you with a hole in your soul that drains you of peace and purpose. If you claim to be a follower of Jesus, this book will help you take an honest look at your faith. Is it rooted in a living relationship with the infinite-personal God, or is it only a fragile system of beliefs driven by conformity and guilt? And if you're not a follower of Jesus, reading this will help you determine if the threads you've chosen are strong enough to keep you secure and steady all the way from here to—and through—eternity.

I've learned so much since stepping into a relationship with Jesus. I've had formal training in the Bible and the Christian faith, read hundreds of great books, and had the privilege of sitting under gifted teachers. But that's not what this book is about. Rather, it's a journal of my discovery of the wonderful reality of God that has grown over a fifty-year friendship of walking with Him through the unfiltered chaos of planet earth. These invisible threads have formed the underlying fabric of my life.

My reading of the Bible over the years has helped me to grow in my understanding of God: how He thinks, acts, reacts, and loves. It has shaped the boundaries of what I can expect from Him and what I can't—of who He is and who He isn't. And although this can sound a bit academic and heady, it's on the canvas of everyday life that the unmistakable realities of the all-loving creator-God are painted and lived.

The pages that follow will chronicle a mixture of personal experience and Biblical understanding. And while experience can never create truth, it can help to validate it. These are not communicated to give any illusion that I've arrived, but to demonstrate how our great God continues to reveal Himself in the story of our lives.

While this book is not intended to be a theological study, it would be less than honest if I didn't acknowledge it is filled with theology. After all, it's our understanding of God that frames our choices and the writing of our story. You may at times find theological positions you don't fully embrace, but that's to be expected since there are many wise and learned people who differ. But don't get lost in the sauce of differences. Move past them in a way that allows you to step into and experience the wonder of God.

My nearly five decades of following Jesus have taken me far more places than I can record in a single volume. I have lived through disappointments and perplexities that are still with me to this day. I have been to heights that have thrilled my soul, and to lows I was sure would end my story. But I've experienced the presence and friendship of God again and again. Today these invisible threads have woven themselves into a tapestry that is strong and durable.

This book is about those threads. While I'll be speaking of them individually for the purpose of explanation, they can only be understood when seen as the weaving of a single fabric. And since each thread is so interwoven with the others, you will find them intersecting throughout the chapters.

We only get one shot at life, and the clock is ticking. It's time for followers of Jesus to stop living as victims of our world's chaos and begin walking with God in the story He has for them. It's what we all want and what Jesus invites us to join. And that's one invitation we can't afford to miss.

Ron Tewson

Chapter One

I'M RESPONSIBLE FOR ME

We all love to play the blame game. It takes little effort and we're pretty good at it.

Woe is me.
Life isn't fair.
It's not my fault.
The cards are all stacked against me.

I'm a poor chess player, yet I've always been fascinated by the game's complexity: sixteen pieces—pawns, rooks, bishops, knights, castles, queen, and the all-important king. It's all about working a strategy to take out my opponent's king while at the same time making sure mine is protected. And if I lose, or *when* I lose, it's nobody's fault but mine. In my quest to win I failed to protect the king. Checkmate: game over.

We humans are an incredibly complex species with intellects off the charts and bodies that can be honed to accomplish incredible feats. Yet at our core is something that holds the key to everything: the king. It's not the intellect, and it's not the body. It's the soul: that invisible, weightless central processing system that is the command center of who we are and all that matters to us. And when it goes down, its checkmate: game over.

This means our number one responsibility in the game of life is to make sure our souls are healthy and protected. If we don't, we can't blame the economy, our family of origin, friends, relatives, health, or our job. It's one hundred percent on us.

The Soul

We're first introduced to the soul in the opening chapters of the Bible. After God had completed His marvelous creation, we read this:

> *Then God said, "Let Us make mankind in **Our image,** according to **Our likeness…***
>
> Genesis 1:26

> *…Then the Lord God formed the man of dust from the ground and breathed into his nostrils the breath of life; **and the man became a living soul.***
>
> Genesis 2:7

This was something very different from the life He had already created because it had a spiritual component. The soul—the God-breathed core of who we are—is what integrates body, mind, and spirit and connects us to our creator. Living in these three interconnected dimensions has everything to do with what it means to be created in the image of God. It's what drives the deep longing in each of us for a life of peace and purpose.

But when we fail to keep the soul healthy, it gets exhausted and parched. We feel alone and vulnerable as things begin to bother us more than they should. We find it difficult to make decisions, even simple ones. Our judgment suffers and it's harder to resist impulses we know aren't good for us. We experience apathy, shame, self-absorption, toxic anger, feelings of depression, insecurity, panic, meaninglessness, and the loss of relationships. This is not the life we want, nor is it the one God intended for us.

Jesus was a soul specialist and had a lot to say about its health:

> *Come to Me, all you who are weary and burdened, and I will give you rest. Take My yoke upon you and learn from Me, for I'm gentle and humble in heart, and you will find rest for your souls. For My yoke is easy and My burden is light.*
>
> Matthew 11:28-30

Does that sound good or what!? The call is to any who are weary and burdened, and the promise is for all who long for rest.

The yoke Jesus is talking about here is a wooden harness that connects animals for work. It's frequently used with oxen for pulling plows, carts, and wagons.

Jesus is saying that if we're yoked to Him—connected to Him—it changes everything because He's pulling with us. In fact, He's pulling *more* than we are so we don't get crushed by the intense weight of the world. This is how God designed it to work from the very beginning. He never intended for anyone to have to navigate the chaos of this planet without Him. It's way too hard.

Our tendency is to think that a restful soul can only be experienced when the stars are perfectly aligned: health, work, and our relational worlds are firing on all cylinders. Our political party is running the government, the stock market is moving up, and the kids are moving out.

But that's far from what Jesus is saying: our world is not that kind or friendly. We'll be looking at this more in Chapter Four. Life is complicated and, while we don't like to hear it, some of our circumstances may never change. The money is gone, the relationship is over, and the disease has taken its irreversible toll.

Ease and *rest* are soul words: living with a divine rhythm that births an inner sense of peace and purpose, even in adverse circumstances. But this can only be experienced when the soul is healthy. If we fail to protect it, every arrow draws blood and the smallest pebble tips the scale. The king is in trouble and the game's outcome is in jeopardy.

The Starting Point

So how do we develop and maintain a healthy soul that lives with a deep sense of ease and rest? That's what this entire book is about, but let's start at the beginning.

The other week I was away at a cabin several hours from home and discovered I needed an adapter to connect my computer to the internet. Once I purchased it, I figured all I'd have to do is plug and play. But when I opened the box, I was greeted with a bright red sticker: *STOP! Run the installation CD first before connecting this device.* I had the part, but it had to be activated before it would work.

The soul needs to be activated to be healthy and at rest. The wonderful living souls God had created in His image took a fatal hit when the very first people, Adam and Eve, chose to raise their own flag and vote God off the island. They weren't convinced He had their best interests in mind and wanted to do things their way. So they walked away from the God who loved them and the connection was lost. This disconnect is what's at the root of the deep unrest people continue to experience, telling them something is missing and not right. As Saint Augustine prayed in the fifth century, "Thou hast formed us for Thyself, and our hearts are restless till they find rest in Thee."

So how do we activate the soul? First, the bad news: we can't do it on our own. Our choice to reject God in our actions, thoughts, and words—things the Bible calls sin—created a massive separation that makes the connection impossible. The gap is just too big. No matter how hard we try—and try and try and try—we still find ourselves falling far short of earning enough gold stars to merit the favor of a holy God.

But here's the good news: God can do what we can't. That's what the cross of Jesus Christ is all about. Driven by His relentless love, He paid the awful price of death to bridge the separation created by our sin. He then offers forgiveness and a forever relationship with Him as a gift. This means it's possible for every person to be made whole as He breathes His love and life into their dead souls.

The first step in having a healthy soul is receiving the gift He's paid for and makes available to everyone. Jesus has done all He can, and if we choose to walk away from His love, it's on us. But if we agree with Him about our sin—that the cross is our only hope— and joyfully take the gift He offers, the barrier of sin is removed and our souls come alive. It's our choice. Here's how the Bible describes it:

> *The wages* (penalty) *of sin is death* (separation from God), *but the free gift of God is eternal life* (the life of God) *through Jesus Christ our Lord.*
>
> Romans 6:23

This is what the Bible refers to as being "born again." It makes sense, doesn't it? Our dead souls coming alive in the love of God.

Soul Care

But once we've done this, it doesn't take long to discover that the realities of life can mess with the divine connection. Stress, deadlines, and the endless pressure to keep all the plates spinning has a way of disrupting the airwaves. It's like being in a place with poor cell service:

- The connection is there but unclear
- You only catch every third word
- There is a lot of static
- Calls get dropped

When this happens at the soul level, you begin to feel on edge, distracted, frustrated, and alone. Your soul is alive, yet you experience an uneasy sense of distance and are in need of the fresh breath of God. The writer of Proverbs cautioned about this many years ago:

Above all else, guard your heart, for everything you do flows from it.

Proverbs 4:23 NIV

The Bible interchangeably uses the words *heart* and *soul* to define this critical operating system of our lives. Guarding it is to take priority over everything. Just like in the game of chess, all the pieces of our lives need to be arranged to protect our souls. If we don't, it's checkmate: game over.

Being Intentional

We're not nearly as good at taking responsibility for our soul's health as we are at the blame game. We allow the tyranny of the urgent—work, family, finances, entertainment, kids' birthday parties, sports, home projects, even church—to control our lives and drain the vitality from our souls. We run like hamsters on a wheel as we cry, "We're just so busy." Yet much of our busyness is nothing more than self-imposed complications we've introduced by the mismanagement of our lives. We're just not serious about protecting the king.

One of the critical threads I've worked hard to weave into the fabric of my life is to make sure my schedule is oriented around soul health. I've incorporated a number of non-negotiable practices, with great intentionality, that I've been doing for decades. Even though it's neither easy nor convenient, I've learned there's way too much at stake to live with a depleted soul.

I'm going to share a few of my practices here, not so you can copy them—although you are certainly welcome to do so—but to help you begin thinking creatively about how you can arrange the unique rhythm of your life to keep your soul healthy and at rest. The primary principle that drives what I do is a simple one:

Be still and know that I am God.

Psalm 46:10

Slowing and *Knowing*

Life screams at us with a noise level that's deafening. Years ago it was only the stationary invaders of television and radio, but today the noise is mobile and endless. Earbuds have become part of the human anatomy. It's not that all the noise is bad, because it's not. The problem is that it's constant! And unless we intentionally choose to unplug and reduce the RPMs, the voice of God will get drowned out. King David, a man who experienced the peace and purpose of God in life's chaos, understood this and recorded his practice:

> *My soul, wait in silence for God only, for my hope is from Him.*
>
> Psalm 62:5

I like that: he took charge of his soul's health. So do I. Every morning I make the very intentional choice to take the first thirty minutes of my day to *slow* and *know*: to unplug, turn down the decibels, clear my schedule, be still, and engage with God.

It starts in a chair that is away from the activities going on in my home. I don't sit at my desk because it's filled with unfinished tasks and a computer that is eager to interrupt my thoughts.

My phone stays in another room; I'm not there to hear from others or catch up on what's trending. I can do that later. This is my time to restore my soul by being still and hearing from God. I have too much going on in my day, too many people depending on me, and too many decisions to make to risk doing it with an unhealthy soul.

I close the door and begin thanking God for the incredible ways He's blessed me. I've learned that the quickest way to a sick soul is ungratefulness, so I start by recounting the good things, one by one. While there are certainly things I'm not grateful for, I am so blessed! Before long I'm filled with a sense of calm and appreciation.

Then I open my Bible and begin reading. I don't do this randomly but usually a book or section at a time. *I'm never in a hurry*! It's not a race to read through the Bible in a year or to put a check on some reading plan. It's a time to open myself up to God so He can breathe His life and love into my needy soul. Sometimes I only get through a few verses because something in the words grabs my heart, and other times several chapters. It's the fostering of a very enjoyable relationship with the living God as I'm refreshed in who He is. We'll talk more about this in Chapter Seven.

When I've finished the reading piece—or sometimes right in the middle if something has sparked a thought—I begin talking with God about what's going on in my life: my fears, anxieties, perplexities, and concerns:

Trust in Him at all times, O people; Pour out your heart before Him; God is a refuge for us.

Psalm 62:8

Not a dribble, but a pouring. I ask Him to step in and solve some things, for the right perspective and response to things that are concerning me, and for insight into decisions I need to make. Sometimes I openly complain about whatever, which is perfectly legal because God has big shoulders. If I don't, I know I'll end up complaining to those around me, which is downright wrong and damaging.

And I listen. I always have something to write on so I don't forget the impressions God is giving me. Sometimes it's answers to things I've been praying about. Sometimes it's a challenge about things I should start or stop doing. Sometimes it's a perspective or idea I've never even thought of before. And sometimes it's a downright correction. OUCH! But it's real, it's alive, and I get refreshed. It's a great way to start my day before stepping into the world of noise.

Then every week I have another practice I've been doing for decades. It's usually on my day off because I have more discretionary time. I extend my *slow and know* time to at least an hour. In addition to my daily practices, I often journal my thoughts from the previous week or read something that expands my understanding of God and His ways.

Once again, the goal is never to just check something off a list but to allow the *knowing* of God to restore my soul. I need to be reminded again and again that God is actively engaged in my life, is for me, loves me, and I'm never alone.

About four times a year I escape to the woods for an overnighter. I'm an outdoors guy and there's something about being alone in the stillness of the forest that refreshes my soul. During my pastoring days, I'd leave after the service on Sunday and return Monday in time for dinner. I pitch my tent, light a fire, and enjoy twenty-four hours of solitude with no human voices (no cell service). I read my Bible, pray, write, read a book or two I've brought, organize, plan, and feel a very real sense of the joy and presence of my heavenly Father.

Then at least once a year—twice if I can—I leave the city and head to a mountain cabin for a week away from everyone, including family. My phone is off and there are no emails, texts, or social media. And no people. It's not a vacation but a time to make sure my soul is healthy and I'm heading in the right direction. I don't want to spend my life climbing a ladder, only to get to the top and discover it's leaning against the wrong building. I often find myself praying the words of King David:

Search me, O God, and know my heart; Try me and know my anxious thoughts; and see if there be any hurtful way in me, and lead me in the everlasting way.

Psalm 139:23-24

I have extended times in the Bible that can go on for several uninterrupted hours. I have increased times of prayer, often pacing on a back deck overlooking the mountains where I laugh, cry, sing, complain, rejoice, reflect, repent, yell, and pour out my heart to God in a way that is unfiltered and authentic. I'm constantly journaling and writing my thoughts. I always take at least a dozen books that focus on a wide range of God-centered topics: sometimes I read several, sometimes none.

And I always take whiteboards. I write thoughts, questions, and impressions as I pray and read because I want to keep them in front of me. Some of the clearest leadings from God that have changed the course of my life have come from these extended times away. My soul is restored, the divine connection is clear, and the presence and leading of God is unmistakable.

I'm often asked when I return from these times away if I had fun. My response usually goes something like this: "Well, it's kind of like remodeling a house. You start with great ideas, but when you take down a wall and discover termite damage, the job gets a whole lot bigger. Now I have to fix the problem before I can build."

It seems that whenever I take extended times alone with my best friend, He lovingly reveals termite damage: bitterness, unforgiveness, selfishness, and carelessness. And while I want to overlook these and move on, He won't let me because He knows it will eventually rot my soul. I don't call that fun. But in the long run it builds me stronger, better, more secure, and more in love with the God who loves me.

Busyness that Chokes

I'm sure about now some of you are thinking, "That sounds so good. I wish I had the time to do something like that, but I'm just too busy." I understand this because I often feel the same way. But then I realize it's nothing more than playing the blame game and not taking responsibility for something that's one hundred percent on me.

Of course there have been times I've had to make adjustments because of life's interruptions. Yet this is something I've done in the seasons of raising five children, starting companies, working several jobs while starting churches, and now developing a new organization. It's only happened because I've planned with *great intentionality* to arrange the pieces of my life around making sure my soul is healthy. My life and the lives of those around me depend on it, and it's the same for you.

I have no question you're busy; you should be. But in your busyness, don't fail to protect the king. Keep your practices fresh and meaningful because there is no magic in rote performance. Figure out a rhythm that works for you and then get intentional about making it happen.

Jesus told the story of a farmer who scattered seed that landed on four different kinds of soil. He later explained the meaning to His disciples: the seed was His life-giving words, and the soils represented the different effects His words had on the hearers. There was no effect with the first group, the second "soil" showed an initial excitement that quickly faded, and the fourth took root and produced a good crop.

But the one that is the most troubling is the third. This seed landed on good soil, took root, and began to grow. But the weeds and thorns prevented it from producing anything of value. Here's how Jesus explained it:

> *...these are the ones who have heard the word, but the worries of this life, and the deceitfulness of wealth, and the desires for other things enter and choke the word, and it becomes unfruitful.*
>
> Mark 4:18-19

They chose to let the busyness and demands of life choke out what mattered most. In their quest to win, they failed to protect the king.

Preparing for the Big One

Hurricane Michael hit the panhandle of Florida in October of 2018, destroying nearly everything in its path and doing extensive damage to Mexico Beach. As the news networks converged to cover the story, I remember a CNN feature about a house that was still standing when all those around it had been leveled. The first question they asked the owners was, "Why did your house survive?" Their answer told the story:

"We put a lot of work into it. We paid attention to every detail from the ground up. At every point… when it came time to make a decision about what level of material to use…we went above and beyond the code because we asked the question, 'What would survive the big one?', and we consistently tried to build it for that."

The report went on to detail that the house had been built to withstand a wind velocity of over a hundred miles per hour above the Florida Hurricane Code. This increased the cost by more than twenty percent.

It wasn't luck that this house survived. It wasn't because it was hit with lesser winds than the others. *The difference was in the intentionality of the preparation.* They decided not to settle for the minimum but to pay attention to every detail: to go beyond the code and spend more money. In every decision, they asked the same bottom-line question: "What would it take to survive the big one?"

Let me ask you the same question: What are you doing to make sure you survive the big one? For some, it's already hit and your life is reeling. For others it hasn't, but let me assure you—it will; it's only a question of when. It may come in the form of a doctor's report with test results you never saw coming. It may be an economic downturn, unexpected change in employment, or a financial meltdown. It may be a relational heartbreak from divorce, betrayal, abandonment, or death.

I've seen it again and again, and when it hits, some crumble under the force of the winds. They curse God, curse people, and live the remainder of their days bitter, broken, and empty because their souls weren't prepared for the big one. It just wasn't that important.

But I've seen others who, in the same intensity of pain and loss, raise their eyes to heaven and say, "The Lord is my good shepherd. As awful as the winds are, they're not going to destroy me because my soul is refreshed with the breath of the living God." And through the pain they rise again to experience lives of peace, purpose, and hope.

Jesus was clear from the beginning that chaos would be the norm of life in this world. This means it's our responsibility—and ours alone—to do whatever it takes to keep our souls healthy and protected.

- Not to settle for the minimum.
- To go above and beyond the code.
- To pay attention to every detail.

Because if we don't, it's checkmate: game over. And that's just too big of a price to pay with our one and only lives.

I have set the Lord continually before me; Because He is at my right hand, I will not be shaken.

Psalm 16:8

Chapter Two

PLAYING TO AN AUDIENCE OF ONE

A large part of my college training was in music and theater. I still have a deep appreciation for the creativity and real-time challenge of the stage.

I've read plenty of Shakespeare over the years. There's a phrase you've probably heard but may not know comes from a monologue in his play, *As You Like It*: "All the world's a stage, and all the men and women merely players." The character is saying everyone is playing a part in the unfolding drama of life. They enter through birth and exit through death.

So if we're all players on the stage of life, the obvious question is simple yet profound: *Who is the audience?*

One of the things I remember from my theater days is the anxiety I'd feel before every performance. How will I be accepted? Will the audience think I did a good job? Will they like me? I always made sure to have a few there who would be in my corner no matter what.

Then there was the audience of paying patrons who would have differing opinions, depending on their preferences, taste, and how their day was going. It would be a mixed bag.

But the audience that mattered most was the one writing the reviews: the critics. They held the power of the play's future and of me as an actor.

I still remember when I had a leading role in the comedy *The Underpants*. No, we didn't walk around in our underwear, but the reviews might have been better if we had. They were so bad I didn't even want to leave my house the next day. Let's just say that when Steve Martin produced an adaptation of the play on Broadway in 2002, he didn't call me.

But when I had a part in the production of *Little Me*, and it got rave reviews, I walked a little taller. I couldn't wait to make the rounds and hear the joyous refrain of "great job" over and over again. We were stars—the talk of the town. The applause of the critics mattered, and life was good.

Every day we're surrounded by an audience of critics who freely dispense their opinions on everything from money to career, morality, relationships, and what matters most in life. It can be unsettling. Yet we alone have to decide whose applause we're going to play to, and that decision will ultimately write the story of our lives.

A Change of Direction

I figured I could write my own ticket into the future after graduating in the top ten of my high school class of over eight hundred. By twenty-two, I'd performed on stages throughout the United States and over a dozen countries. I'd heard lots of applause and loved it. My academic accomplishments opened other opportunities that could provide me with things I hadn't been able to enjoy growing up.

But then something began to happen in my twenty-third year of life. I can't really explain it, but there was a stirring going on deep in my soul. I'd had the good fortune of growing up in a church that gave me a God-consciousness and kept me from getting too close to the edge. I considered myself a Christian because I *believed* in Jesus and had even tried to convince others to do the same.

Yet this was different. It was beyond an academic understanding of Christianity and very personal. I was single at the time and living alone in a small apartment in Los Angeles where I'd moved to further my career. And there, in the stillness of my little four hundred square foot abode, I began to read the Bible. Not just a quick pick-me-up-feel-good devotional like I'd done in the past, but hours and hours for days and months.

For the first time in my adult life, I found myself overcome by the profound significance of Jesus and what He had done for me. It wasn't that I was a bad guy who needed saving from a lot of bad stuff, because

35

I wasn't. I'd actually made it all the way through college—in the theater department—without ever even smoking a joint! Go figure. But what became so clear to me was that no matter how good I was—even though I was better than a lot of others and proud of it—I was far below the righteous standards of God.

Ah…but then there was Jesus, and the cross, and the things I'd heard for so many years began to take on a new significance. The cross was more than just the central symbol and event of Christianity. It was the act of a loving God who stepped in to meet the demands of His own righteousness: death for sin, MY sin. The cross was His way of bridging the separation and making it possible for me to step into a whole new kind of life. Not a *religious* life, but one that was powered by a very personal and loving relationship with the living God. It sounded too good to be true, but I said, "I'm in. I don't want to just believe in You but follow You—to know and experience You every day of my life." So, at twenty-three years of age, I started on a journey that set me on the course I'm still on today.

Joining God in His Story

The Bible did a lot more than just introduce me to a personal relationship with Jesus, although that would have been enough. It pulled me into the story of God.

I read about Moses, the brilliant city-building engineer who was at the top of his game as part of Egypt's royal family. Then he goes and loses it all by trying to carve out a place for himself in God's story on his own terms. He's forced to flee Egypt with only the clothes on his back and begins to build a new life in a foreign country. It wasn't what he'd imagined for himself, but it was good. He got married, had kids, and was making a good living in the family business.

Then God shows up and gives him the opportunity to risk everything and join Him in His story. He was about to move the people of Israel from slavery in Egypt to their own land and was asking Moses to take the lead. No benefits or relocation package, and no salary guarantee. He got only one promise from God: "I'll be with you."

At that moment, Moses was faced with a huge decision: whose applause was he going to play to? Would it be the one that cheered the building of a kingdom of security, convenience, and upward mobility? Or would he play to an audience of ONE and join God in His story?

It wasn't an easy choice. He'd already tried it once and things hadn't turned out as he'd hoped. He liked where he was in life and gave God every reason why He should pick someone else. But deep in His soul he knew he wanted more, so he chose to play to the bigger audience—an audience of ONE—and it changed his life forever. He chose to play to the ONE who applauded values far different from the ones he'd grown up with and seemed strange to those around him. His name had already been erased from Egyptian history. Would he now die a nameless nomad wandering in the desert?

Yet in the end he had a story to tell that's still being told! The pages of Egyptian history may have forgotten him, but God never did. Today his name is among the most recognized in all the world. He played to the right audience.

But not all who joined Moses on the wilderness journey had the same experience. They started out well, but the increased hardships caused many to seek the applause of safety, security, and an easier life. It was a bad choice. Six hundred thousand of them ended up with no applause at all and died in the desert. They played to an audience that couldn't deliver.

Then I read about a teenager named Daniel and his three friends who were taken captive in the Babylonian invasion of Israel in 605 BC. Their lives were spared because of their brilliance, and they soon found themselves among the elite being trained for the king's service. Life was surprisingly good as they enjoyed living conditions far better than their fellow captives.

But they soon discovered the audience of their new culture would only applaud if they played counter to the ways of the God they followed. Twice they were pushed to the point of death and had to choose their audience, and twice they determined—with unwavering commitment—to play to the audience of ONE. Both times their lives were spared, both times God's purpose was accomplished through them, both times they experienced the joy of God's presence, and both times they ended up with stories we're still telling today: Daniel in a lion's den (Daniel 6), his three friends in a fiery furnace (Daniel 3).

Then there was my favorite: Jesus. He spent forty days alone in the desert just before going public, allowing Satan to take his three best shots at derailing Him from His mission. Each of Satan's temptations focused on a single question: which audience was Jesus going to play to? The narrative is found in chapter four of the Gospel of Matthew.

Satan's first shot was to get Jesus to play to the audience that applauds doing whatever it takes to satisfy your desires and feel good. Since He hadn't eaten for forty days, Satan pushed Him to tap into His divine abilities to satisfy His hunger by making bread from stones. "Use your power to take care of number one and feel good. You don't need to involve your Father in this because You already know all He wants is for You to be happy, happy, happy. Trust Your instincts. Go ahead and do whatever it takes to satisfy Your hunger; if it feels good it must be right, so just do it!" Sound familiar?

His second temptation was to get Jesus to play to the applause of popularity. All He had to do was pull off a spectacular magic trick: jump from the pinnacle of the temple and watch as the angels rushed to catch Him before He hit the ground. Wow…the people would be impressed and flock to Him! He'd again have to sneak this one past His Father because it wasn't part of the master plan. But hey, what's wrong with a little compromise if it makes people like you? After all, the end justifies the means, right?

His final shot was to get Jesus to play to the thunderous applause that comes from power. People love this one; to be seen as powerful and important. Satan promised Jesus all the kingdoms of the world if He would just forget about playing to the applause of His Father and join his team.

Satan was offering Jesus everything He'd eventually have through the cross, but without all the pain. This shortcut sounds good to many of us: all the upside without the downside. But the benefits are only illusionary because Satan can never deliver on his promises.

Jesus responded with the ways and words of His Father in each of these temptations. He wasn't going to play to any other applause because He trusted His Father implicitly. He had already determined that playing to an audience of ONE was far more important than all the others combined. It was a choice that changed the world—and changed me.

Choosing an Audience of ONE

As my little twenty-three-year-old brain struggled to process all this, I knew I had to make a choice: what audience was I going to play to? And there in the quietness of my little home, I made the decision to play to the grander audience—an audience of ONE. Although I had little understanding of how this would affect my future, I made it just the same. And it's a thread that has run through my life ever since.

Even as I write these words, I remember the incredible sensation I felt—really for the first time—that I was truly free! No longer did I have to play to the expectations of my peers, my family, the people at work, or the success image. No longer did I have to try and get God to like me because He already did and would be in my corner—always. I was now playing to a new audience, an audience of ONE, and that gave me the freedom to look at my future through an entirely different lens.

It wasn't long after this that I asked Joy to marry me. I took her to my little place that was furnished with state-of-the-art curbside and garage sale pieces and told her the craziest thing: We may never have any more than this because I'm not going to play to the audience that says you are what you own. Yeah, I know, I have a way with women. But maybe the even crazier thing is that she said yes!

A few months after our wedding we moved from California to Texas to join some who were planting a new church near the University of Houston. I needed to find a paying job so, with my great resume as an international performer, I was able to get work picking up trash at the large apartment complex where we lived. The lack of applause was deafening! My brother and I started a roofing company the following year and our financial future began to look promising.

But as I continued to pray about the part God had for us in His story, we found ourselves in conversations about starting a church at Texas A&M University in College Station. This was scary because it would mean leaving my growing business and moving where I'd have no income. We had one child at the time and another on the way. The audience screaming in my head that cheered increased security and upward mobility said absolutely no: pure craziness. Don't even think about it.

Yet the more we engaged the audience of ONE, the more we felt a nudge…a whisper…another nudge… and then a green light to co-lead this team. Within a few months we'd packed up and made the move with a dozen others. Joy and I rented a small unairconditioned house in the middle of the summer, and although it was hot—*very* hot—it was perfectly located only three blocks from the campus.

We stored our food in ice-chests for the first few months because we didn't have a refrigerator or the money to buy one. We frequently had little in the cupboards and even less in our bank account. But life change was happening as more and more students were coming into an authentic relationship with Jesus. That little house—where we moved the furniture from the living room to the front yard twice a week to create more space—became the holy ground where the community of those experiencing the love of Jesus continued to meet and grow. It was an incredible time as we sensed the applause of God.

An Unexpected Change

Then things hit the fan. After several years, my co-pastor felt it would be best for him and his young family to move to Austin to be closer to relatives, which they did. This meant I would now be responsible for leading this young church alone. The thought was overwhelming. Things were already hard, and it would make perfect sense to close up shop and move to a more secure place. No one would blame us; some would even applaud. But what did the audience of ONE think? I didn't know.

Feeling alone and hopeless, I packed a few things into my car—tent, sleeping bag, water—and headed two hours east to the Davey Crocket National Forest. I told Joy I'd be back within a month because I wasn't taking any food. All I knew was that I wasn't coming home until I was sure I'd heard from the ONE we were committed to following.

The next eight days were spent roaming the woods—far from any living person—yelling, complaining, crying, and shouting to God that this wasn't fair. "There's not enough leadership for this church to keep going. There's not enough money. I don't have enough time or skill. I can't do this."

Those days took me to a new place in my understanding of what it means to play to an audience of ONE. Deep in the woods, I heard the unmistakable whisper of God. "Ron, you're My masterpiece. You're MY masterpiece. I created you. I love you. I delight in

43

You. You're right where I want you to be and you're not alone. Don't listen to the naysayers and critics telling you what My church should look like. Never forget that My heart is for redeeming and restoring the people I love, and that's what you're doing. If you keep following My heart—if you keep playing to Me and not to all the voices around you—you'll get My applause."

I came back from the woods and, to this day, have never looked back. That church continued to grow and is still flourishing today. A couple of years ago I had the opportunity to speak at their men's conference that included two churches they'd started in nearby cities. And as I looked across a room filled with lives that had been changed by the redeeming power of the love of Jesus, I was reminded of just how close I'd come to playing to the wrong audience and missing what God had for me in His story. It was very humbling.

Following the Applause

Several years later I was asked if I would consider relocating to New Mexico to help a small church that was struggling. This made no sense because I loved what I was doing, loved the city, and the church was healthy and growing. The New Mexico church couldn't pay me a thing and we'd have to find our own place to live. It sounded like a definite thumbs down.

Yet the more we engaged the audience we were committed to playing to, the more the whispers kept coming: "Go, Go, Go"…But, But, But…"Go, Go, Go." So Joy and I and our now four children, ten and under, took off for Albuquerque.

After a couple of short nomadic stays we settled into a small two-bedroom house; Joy and I in one room, the four kids in the other. I know…first-world child abuse! Just for fun we added a dog and a few chickens. That church not only survived but grew and went on to start other churches in the years that followed. And as we look back, we all have stories to tell because that's what happens when you play to an audience of ONE.

Our next move took us to a growing church in the Washington, DC, area. But after several years, we began to feel the distinct nudge to leave vocational ministry and move to Central Florida to be close to my aging parents. This seemed strange because it was a significant shift from the way God had been leading us over the years. Once again I wouldn't have a job, and we'd be unable to purchase a home until ours in Maryland sold. But the whisper turned into a shout, and we made the move.

As you can imagine, we ended up with stories to tell of the goodness and faithfulness of God. In addition to caring for my parents until their deaths, I was able to start a good business that created financial stability for our family.

Then that unsettling nudge began to again move in my soul. The longer I was in the business community, the more I felt the need for a church that had an energy around God's heart for those far from Him at its core. And so it started. Small at first as I continued to work my business, but as that little church grew, I knew I would have to choose one or the other.

This was hard because I loved the applause and affirmation I was getting from the secure world I'd created. I loved the perks that came with success and I loved the pace of life I was experiencing. Was God asking me to close the door on all this and walk away—to risk what I'd worked so hard to build? The answer came loud and clear: Yes. But it also came with the promise I needed: *We'll do it together.*

This meant an income reduction and lifestyle adjustment. But people were coming into an authentic relationship with Jesus, lives were changing, and I could hear the divine applause as I fell into bed at night.

Our once-a-week rented facility was limiting, and we knew we'd need a more functional location to step into the next phase of integrating into our community. So we launched a capital campaign to raise the necessary funds, and many stepped up and gave sacrificially. But now Joy and I had a decision to make: what were we going to give?

We'd already walked away from most of our financial security and I was getting older. The audience of caution echoing in my head—the one that cheers the protecting of your kingdom above all else—suggested a reasonable amount. But the audience of ONE gave us another number that was anything but reasonable. Really, God? Are You serious!?

We went with the second and have stories to tell. Today we live debt-free in a wonderful home with furnishings from places other than curbsides and garage sales. The church was able to secure space in an old K-Mart building in the heart of town and continues to be a beacon of the love of God in the community.

Finishing Strong

As I write these words, I am more aware than ever that we live in a time when there is less and less applause for those who dare to stand on the side of Jesus and His ways. We are continually pressured to cave to the applause of cultural, political, and even religious correctness. But what I've learned on my journey with God is that playing to an audience of ONE is the only way to stay in the game and finish strong. While the other applauses are enticing and enjoyable in the moment, they never last.

Playing to the divine audience means you may never hear earthly applause for the things you've done. It may even go—intentionally and unintentionally—to others. I've experienced it countless times and don't like it. Yet in the end, it deepens my commitment to continue playing to the ONE who keeps impeccable records and never misses a thing.

Over the years of disappointments, criticisms, wins, losses, misunderstandings, successes, financial shortfalls and windfalls, it's been the audience of ONE that has reminded me of who I am: a masterpiece of

God, loved by my creator and invited to join Him in His story. And if I'd be willing to play to His applause, He'd walk with me through every challenge and continue to breathe life into my weary soul.

Then the day will come when I'll step off the world stage and find myself standing before an audience of only ONE. And as His thunderous applause echoes through the heavens, I'll know I made the right choice.

And I'll have stories to tell for all eternity.

Whom have I in heaven but You? And besides You, I desire nothing on earth. My flesh and my heart may fail, but God is the strength of my heart and my portion forever.
                                    Psalm 73:25-26

Chapter Three

GOD IS ALWAYS UP TO SOMETHING

I walked from my home on the afternoon of March 30, 1981, to visit friends living on the next street. I arrived to find their front door open and, as I looked through the screen, I could see them all gathered around the television. A little odd for the middle of the day. I was soon to learn there had been an assassination attempt on the life of President Ronald Reagan.

He'd been in office only a few months and had just finished a speech at the Washington Hilton in Washington, DC. As he approached his waiting limousine, several gunshots came from the sidewalk. It had happened just a short time before I'd gotten there.

I returned home and, like everyone else in the country, was glued to my television for the rest of the day. We tuned into ABC and watched as Frank Reynolds, the news anchor, worked to keep up with the fragments of information as they streamed into his earpiece. It was sketchy at best. Word was that several had been shot, one being Press Secretary James Brady. Yet Reynolds assured everyone that the President was OK: "Word is that the President has not been hit."

Then he stopped. "Wait. What was that? Word is that the President has been hit. He HAS been hit." Reynolds was visibly shaken. "What we've been reporting to you is not right. The President has been shot." His trembling voice went on to inform the viewers that James Brady, a personal friend, had died from his wound.

After repeating the details several more times, he again stopped: "Wait a minute! Word is now that he has not died after all. He HAS NOT died after all." And then, in one of the classic moments of network television news history, the emotional Frank Reynolds blurted, "Let's get it nailed down! Somebody, let's find out. Let's get it straight so we can report this thing accurately." The network quickly went to a commercial break.

He was angered and frustrated with having insufficient information to make sense of what was happening.

Being in a Better Story

I've felt like Frank Reynolds more times than I can count. Something unsettling is going on in my little world, yet there are only disconnected fragments of information. It can push me to the edge.

We're all up to something all the time. We live planned lives that revolve around the story we're writing—one affectionately known as *The Story of Me*. And when things mess with our story it creates anxiety, conflict, and irritation. We want to get things nailed down *right now* so we can connect the dots and get on with the narrative. But there's a problem in all this: We've forgotten whose story we're in.

The Bible opens with the words, "In the beginning, God…." The story God is writing doesn't begin with you or me. It doesn't read, "In the beginning, Ron…." I'd like that because then I'd be the main character, large and in charge. But it doesn't. It's His story.

What we see from the start is that God is always up to something. The first thing we see Him doing is creating a wonderful stage for His story to be played out on: land, water, heavenly bodies, light, darkness, plant and animal life. Then, when everything is just as He wants it, He adds His true masterpiece: people—living souls created in His image. All is good.

But it didn't take long, as we saw in Chapter One, for people to grab the pen from God and shout, "Mine, Mine! This is going to be MY story and I'M going to be the main character. Maybe I'll give God a bit part—if He's lucky—but make no mistake. It's going to be *The Story of Me*, large and in charge."

What do you think happens when you have billions of people all writing their own story with themselves as the main character? Chaos; everyone wants to control the game board. And when people or circumstances get in the way, it fuels anger, frustration, exhaustion, broken relationships, and pain.

This breaks the heart of God. So He introduces a new plot-line into His story that is all about *redemption*. The Bible is the unfolding story of His redemptive plan to pull those He loves back into a trusting relationship with Him. Only then can they experience the life of peace and purpose He designed for them from the beginning.

It's important to understand that redemption isn't about God *taking* what doesn't belong to Him. Not even close. It's about Him *getting back* what has always been His. Just like finding something in a pawn shop that you've had taken, a price has to be paid to get it back. It holds a special value to you and, even though it's rightfully yours, you are willing to take the loss.

That's what the cross is all about: Jesus taking the loss by paying the price of death to buy us back—or *redeem* us—so we can be restored to our place in His story. The sequence of Ephesians 2:8-10 (NLT) is one of my favorites in its description of this:

> *God saved you by His grace when you believed. And you can't take credit for this; it is a gift from God. Salvation is not a reward for the good things we have done, so none of us can boast about it. For we are God's masterpiece. He has created us anew in Christ Jesus, so we can do the good things He planned for us long ago.*

I'm God's masterpiece. You're God's masterpiece. My little dog is adorable, a good companion, and a wonderful creation of God. But he's not His masterpiece. That title is reserved for you and me alone. When we step into a relationship with God through the cross of Jesus, something incredible happens that changes everything:

> *Therefore, if anyone is in Christ, this person is a new creation; the old things passed away; behold, new things have come.*
>
> 2 Corinthians 5:17

This sounds so good, but what's the point of being a new creation? Is it so we can now get on with our own stories with fewer interruptions until we finally relocate to heaven? Is it so we can now have God on our team to remove all the obstacles standing in our way so we can pursue whatever we want with a guarantee of success? No! It's so we can enter into the *something* God has had for us in HIS story from the very beginning. That's what new creations do; they join God in His story. We'll look at this more in Chapter Five.

But there's a complication. Sometimes we lack sufficient information to know what that *something* is, and it can lead to the Frank Reynolds syndrome: "Let's get it nailed down! Somebody, let's find out. Let's get it straight so we can report this thing accurately." It can be frustrating and unsettling.

Learning to Trust

One of the first things Jesus did when He began to go public was gather a handful of disciples: twelve. It would be up to them to continue everything He was about to start after He was gone. But it would only work if they trusted Him. They had to have the confidence that He knew what He was doing—even when they didn't—and that He'd always have their back. If they didn't, they'd keep inserting their own agendas and eventually go back to writing their own stories.

That's why we find Jesus constantly exposing them to situations where He knows exactly what He's up to, but they don't have a clue. They lack sufficient information and it puts them on edge. They had to learn to trust.

One day Jesus is speaking to a crowd on the shores of Lake Gennesaret while Peter and his fishing partners are cleaning their nets. When He finishes His talk, He asks Peter to throw his freshly cleaned nets into the boat because they're going out into the deep water to catch some fish! This makes absolutely no sense to Peter. He and his crew had caught nothing the night before, and any fisherman worth his salt knows midday fishing is the worst. You can read about this in the opening verses of Luke 5.

Jesus was up to something, but Peter had no idea what it was. He'd already cleaned his nets for the upcoming night's work, and it would mean having to do it all over again. This seemed like a foolish request on Jesus' part and a huge waste of his time.

Yet even with His questioning, Peter navigated his boat out into the lake. The result was not only a massive catch of fish, but a soul awakening that changed him forever. It all started when Jesus was up to something and asked Peter to join Him, even though there wasn't enough information to make sense of it. He was building Peter's trust.

I often hear people say how wonderful they think it must have been to be one of Jesus' early followers in real time. I disagree. I think it would have been very unsettling because He was always pushing them out of their comfort zone. Lots of people liked the free-lunch-get-your-body-healed Jesus, but when He challenged them to join Him in things they didn't understand—to actually trust Him—many checked out.

A little later Jesus is speaking to a crowd of over five thousand out in the country. As it's getting late, He turns to one of His disciples and says:

"Where are we to buy bread so that these people may eat?"

John 6:5

They do some quick calculating and come up with a figure that's way out of the budget, and that's for everyone to only get a snack. They see a kid walking around with a sack lunch of bread and a few dried fish, but don't give it a second thought. The narrative continues:

This He was saying to test him, for He Himself knew what He was intending to do.

John 6:6

He then asks His guys to divide the people into groups of fifties and hundreds and have them sit on the grass: lunch is about to be served! I'm sure they had to be thinking, "Why should we waste our precious time organizing thousands of people into groups, which is no small task, when there is no food!?"

God was up to something, but they didn't have enough information to understand what it was. Would they trust Jesus on this or walk away as so many others had done? But when Jesus begins to multiply the kid's lunch and gives it to them to hand out, they suddenly find themselves part of something so much bigger than their own little stories. All they had to do was trust Jesus—that He was up to something good, even when they couldn't make sense of it.

When Jesus gets word that one of His good friends is seriously sick in another town, He doesn't pick up His pace one bit. He finally arrives in Bethany four days later to find that Lazarus has died, the funeral is over, and his embalmed body lies in the family tomb. Jesus had given His disciples a clue a few days earlier that He was up to something when He said:

...Lazarus is dead, and I am glad for your sakes that I was not there, so that you may believe.

John 11:14-15

Kind of a spoiler alert, but it went right over their heads. They didn't have a clue as to what He was talking about.

But the delay greatly troubled Lazarus' sisters. Both came right out and told Jesus that if He'd only come quicker, their brother would still be alive. If He had just been a little more considerate, paid closer attention, and been a better friend there would have been no need for a funeral. They were upset.

Jesus was up to something, yet their lack of information created a deep sense of confusion, anger, and grief. There was no question He could have healed Lazarus had He gotten there earlier. But what they didn't understand was that He was working a plan far bigger than anything they had ever imagined. When He tells the sisters to have the stone removed from the tomb's entrance, and their brother walks out alive, they realize Jesus knew what He was doing the whole time. And because they were with Him, they got to be part of the story!

As the news of the Bethany resurrection spread, everyone wanted to get a glimpse of the miracle worker. Cheering crowds lined the road a few days later when He entered Jerusalem, and His disciples found themselves part of the biggest show in town!

They had grown up intending to be authors of their own stories and to make them as good as they could. Then they'd met Jesus and He'd invited them into His. It was a risk. But it didn't take long for them to discover that His story was so much more interesting than theirs, was being played out on a bigger stage, and was just plain better. But within a few days their world would be rocked to the core.

Thursday evening was special as they gathered to celebrate the Passover meal together. But when they later walked to a garden, things went terribly wrong. An angry mob appeared from the darkness, arrested Jesus, and took Him to the Jewish leaders for a long night of interrogation. The next morning found Him in front of the Roman authorities, and before the sun set that night, His lifeless body had been carried from a cross and laid in a tomb. It had taken less than twenty-four hours for everything they'd hoped and believed to come crashing down. He wasn't really large and in charge after all: Rome was.

Today we know that God was up to something, but in real time it didn't make a bit of sense. Their daring to trust Him had completely altered their lives. Some had walked away from good jobs, others had relocated, and they'd all numbered themselves with the one who was now considered a threat by the civil and religious authorities. Would there be a price on their heads? Would they even be able to find employment? Would they have to relocate for the safety of their families?

As the sun rose the next morning, it was destined to be the worst day of their lives because it was the day nothing happened. NOTHING. It was that awful in-between day of silence and confusion: they lacked sufficient information to make sense of what was happening.

Yet God was up to something in the silence: Sunday was coming. Women returning from the cemetery at daybreak reported the stone had been rolled from the tomb's entrance—and the body was gone! Peter and John went to the grave and found it as they'd been told. Soundbites of information continued to trickle in throughout the day, and then word began to circulate that the women had both seen and spoken with Jesus. As His closest followers gathered later that night to piece together the fragments, Jesus appeared. He ate and talked with them, and at that moment, they found their very ordinary lives intersecting the greatest story ever told.

But there was one who missed the celebration. He had been excited at the beginning and saw a lot of upside in following Jesus. He was a people mover, shook up the establishment, and challenged the authorities. He liked that. But now the story had taken a twist and wasn't going the way he thought it should. He couldn't make sense of it all so he lost hope, walked away, and sold out for 30 pieces of silver. When Sunday came, Judas wasn't there to see it because he'd ended his life just a few hours earlier. He had gotten so close—but missed it.

Saturdays

One of the threads I've woven into the fabric of my life over the years is that God is always up to something, even when I can't see it. I've learned He's never a passive spectator but an engaged Father who has a special place for me in His story—one that is so much bigger and better than the tiny, insignificant, who-really-cares one I could write for myself.

But I don't like Saturdays. I don't like those in-between days where the lack of information creates uneasiness and confusion because I don't know where the story is going. The silence of Saturdays is filled with perplexity that can lead to despair, especially when they seem to go on, and on, and on. There have been days when I've found myself shouting like Frank Reynolds, "Let's get this nailed down. Let's get it straight…." I want things figured out, and I want them figured out NOW!

The Apostle Paul was no stranger to perplexity, yet what he had to say about it has become one of the foundational verses of my life:

> …*we are afflicted in every way, but not crushed; perplexed, but not despairing*…
>
> 2 Corinthians 4:8

What he's talking about here is a perplexity *without* despair that comes from the confidence that God is always up to something and can be trusted. Sunday is coming and His story is still being written. It may not always read the way I think it should because, if it did, then I'd be the author.

When Jesus' followers saw Him alive, they figured the story would now read more like they'd hoped it would. They would finally be ruling alongside Him in the earthly kingdom He was about to establish. But it wasn't to be. While their story would continue to intersect with His, it wouldn't be in a palace. Sunday meant their lives were about to get a lot more complicated, and it meant that each of them would eventually be killed or exiled for the part they played.

But it was a better story. It was a bigger story. It was a story of adventure and intrigue. It was a story of walking with God and experiencing His presence and power at every turn. It was a story of significance and meaning that left its fingerprints not only on history, but eternity.

Intentional Randomness

When we live with the awareness that God is always up to something, we find ourselves looking for where He might show up next. As I've encountered unforeseen interruptions to my schedule over the years—car trouble, medical issues, things breaking— I've learned to ask, "God, are You up to something? Is there something going on here You want me to engage in? Is there someone You want me to meet?"

I returned to Orlando a few months ago on a late-night flight from the west. Since it was getting in after midnight, I planned to Uber home. I entered the information on my phone when we landed, but my credit card was rejected. I tried Lyft: rejected. I tried another credit card: rejected. What was going on? Very frustrating! After several minutes of growing irritation, I began to calm down and finally said, "OK God, are You up to something?" And as I sat there in the airport at 1:15 in the morning, I committed to living in the story He had for me.

I ended up flagging down a guy who looked a little sketchy, but he had some official-looking sticker in his window so I got in the car. And on the forty-minute trip home, he poured out his heart to me about what was going on in his life. A little weird. When we got to my house I asked if I could pray with him, and when I opened my eyes, tears were streaming down his face. We talked a little more, and then I got out of the car and he drove away. I may never know the outcome of that encounter. Yet as I fell into bed a few minutes later, I did so with a sense that I'd played the part God had for me in touching the life of someone He loves.

Knowing that God is always up to something means we're not at the mercy of random forces but in the hands of our loving Father who is writing our story in a marvelous way. This doesn't mean we'll always understand what He's up to in the moment; it may take weeks, months, or even years. We may never know this side of heaven. But every interruption changes the timeline of history, and the wake of that ripple results in something known only to God.

There was a time when Rome thought they controlled the game board, but then Sunday came. And today, two thousand years later, there are more crosses in the city of Rome than any other city in the world. God is always up to something.

The Good in the Bad

As we close this chapter, let's look at a great verse many followers of Jesus find reassuring in the silence of Saturdays:

And we know that God causes all things to work together for good to those who love God, to those who are called according to His purpose.

Romans 8:28

This is not a guarantee that bad things won't happen, because they will. Nor does it mean that God is the one causing the bad things, because He isn't. Then just what is the *good* the Apostle Paul is talking about? Whatever it is, the promise is only for those who are loving God and committed to living in His purpose. Those who aren't won't be able to recognize the *good* when it comes.

The *good* God is up to is always tied to His bigger story. All too often we want to use this verse as a kind of divine guarantee that something good will happen *to us* out of the bad. And while this is often true, the promise is that something good will happen *in the furthering of God's story.* It's good because it's the better story every follower of Jesus wants to be part of. If we ever lose sight of this, we'll dig ourselves into a hopeless pit of disappointment and, like Judas, miss the glory of Sunday's sunrise.

The author of this verse experienced an endless litany of bad things in living out his part in God's good story. But it was the *knowing* he talked about in Romans 8:28…that God was always up to something good… that gave Him the peace and purpose he enjoyed. Here's what he knew:

> *If God is for us, who is against us?… Christ Jesus is He who died, yes, who rather was raised, who is at the right hand of God, who also intercedes for us. Who will separate us from the love of Christ?… For I am convinced that neither death, nor life, nor angels, nor principalities, nor things present, nor things to come, nor powers, nor height, nor depth, nor any other created thing will be able to separate us from the love of God that is in Christ Jesus our Lord.*
>
> Romans 8:31-39

The *good* was that he could trust the love and presence of God to be consistent in his life, even when he lacked sufficient information to make sense of what was happening. The *good* was that God, even in the confusion, was always up to something good in the writing of His story. And the *good* was that he—once distant from God but now rescued by His grace—got to play a part in it.

And so do we.

> *If I say, "Surely the darkness will overwhelm me, and the light around me will be night," Even the darkness is not dark to You, and the night is as bright as the day. Darkness and light are alike to You.*
>
> Psalm 139:11-12

Chapter Four

THIS IS NOT HEAVEN

Earlier I talked about the wonderful little house we had in Texas. It was great for the size of our family at the time: two bedrooms, kitchen, bathroom, living room, and garage. The only thing it lacked was a quiet space for me to read, think, write, and play my wonderful hand-made guitar. So I took the back part of the garage—connected to the kitchen by a door—put up a wall, and converted it into a study. It was perfect.

Late one night Joy and I were jolted from our sleep by an explosive sound that shook the house. Then it was dead quiet. "Joy," I whispered, "Go see what's going on." No, that's what I wanted to say, but I strapped on my courage and slowly made my way down the short hallway to the kitchen.

As I stood there in the dark, it sounded like there were voices coming from my study. No, couldn't be. I started back to the bedroom, but then figured I should at least open the door and check. And when I did, I found myself staring at a badly wrecked car—still running—with two dazed guys sitting in the front seat. The back wall of the garage was gone.

Within minutes the police were on the scene. They'd been pursuing the car at a hundred miles per hour when it missed the turn, flew through the yard, and crashed into the back of our house. Both the driver and passenger were intoxicated, and a gun rested on the seat between them. Soon the fire department arrived and gave everything a good soaking.

I stood in the ruins of my once delightful study after everyone had left, and it was hard to look at. My desk, file cabinet, bookcase and books were all damaged beyond repair. What the car hadn't destroyed the hundreds of gallons of water did. But the saddest of all was my guitar: the neck was broken and the body smashed. I loved that guitar. It was probably the most valuable thing I owned. Even though insurance reimbursed us for our losses, it was at a time when we didn't have much and had to use the money for other things. I was never able to replace that guitar.

As I picked through the rubble over the next few days, I had to fight off thinking this wasn't right. I'd uprooted my life, walked away from financial security, and inconvenienced my family to help people discover the wonder of Jesus. Soon I found myself in a heated conversation with God: "Come on, is this the best You can do? Why did You let this happen? Couldn't You have at least had the car hit the house next door? Would that have been all that hard? I don't think they even like You." Very confusing. Why would God pick on me when I wanted nothing more than to love Him and pursue the story He had for me?

I know I'm not the only one who has struggled with this. You might be in the middle of it right now. This kind of inner conflict can create tension and deep anger at God, even to the point of some walking away from the faith.

One of the threads I've worked hard to weave into the fabric of my life is just about as basic as you can get: *This is not heaven*. If I ever fall into the trap of thinking it is, I'm setting myself up for a world of disappointment and frustration.

The Old Order

In the final book of the Bible, the author of Revelation talks about things that are to happen in the future. Toward the end, he gives us a glimpse of what he calls *the new heaven and new earth:*

> *He* (Jesus) *will wipe every tear from their eyes. There will be no more death or mourning or crying or pain, for the old order of things has passed away. He who was seated on the throne said, "I am making everything new!"*
>
> Revelation 21:4-5 NIV

This tells us we're living in what he calls the *old order*, one that is characterized by things like death, mourning, crying, and pain. And that order won't come to an end until Jesus makes everything new in heaven. It will never happen on earth. Never.

This can bother some because they think signing on with Jesus somehow exempts them from the realities of being earth-dwellers. Like a get-out-of-jail-free card in the game of Monopoly, it gives them immunity from the misery everyone else has to endure. Then, when they get whacked by the realities of earth dwelling, they accuse God of failing to keep His end of the bargain.

This simply is not true. There is no get-out-of-jail-free card, and no exemption from death, mourning, crying, pain, and the endless chaos of the old order. This is not heaven.

Jesus' final words to His disciples on the night before His crucifixion are recorded in John 14-16. It covers some of His most foundational teachings and concludes with these words:

> *In this world you will have trouble* (distress). *But take heart! I have overcome the world.*
> John 16:33 NIV

He's telling them they shouldn't go around thinking they're not going to have any trouble, because they are. They shouldn't be surprised when the realities of life drop rain on their parade in the form of pain, inconvenience, abuse, and suffering. The ground rules for earth dwelling are relentless and will affect them just as sure as they will everyone else.

And they'll affect us, too. Let's think about a few of these rules.

Life Will Not Always Be Fair

Everyone won't live happily ever after under old-order rules. Stories that end that way are called fairy tales for a reason: it's not how life works in the real world.

Solomon, the son of King David and third king of the nation of Israel, is sometimes referred to as the wisest man who ever lived. He was a poet and philosopher who wrote several Old Testament books, including Proverbs, Ecclesiastes, and the Song of Solomon. He lists a number of things throughout Ecclesiastes that he refers to as *meaningless*, or things that just don't make sense. Here's one of them:

> *There's something else meaningless that occurs on the earth: the righteous who get what the wicked deserve, and the wicked who get what the righteous deserve. This too, I say, is meaningless.*
>
> Ecclesiastes 8:14 NIV

This sounds so wrong, doesn't it? There's something in all of us that says good things should happen to good people and bad things to bad. It just makes sense. That's why when the bad guy in a movie finally gets his comeuppance, the entire theater often erupts in a cheer. We love it when the good guy gets the money, gets the girl, and saves the world. YES! But when it happens the other way around and the bad guy wins, we feel a pit in our stomachs. That's just not the way it should be. But on earth it is: this is not heaven.

The writer of Psalm 73 had a real struggle with this. When he saw all the unfairness going on around him—the wicked getting off easy and the righteous suffering undeserved abuse—he found himself envying the wicked! They rejected God and mistreated people, yet seemed to enjoy lives of prosperity, health, comfort, and ease. He was trying to live a God-honoring life by working hard, being honest, and treating people fairly, yet he was barely making it. Why was this? Simple: this is not heaven. It's all part of the old order.

God Will Not Mastermind Every Action and Reaction on Earth

God is not some kind of interplanetary mystic who spends His days pushing buttons on a galactic super-computer to manipulate the world. Things would look a lot more like heaven if He were. He didn't push a button in 2017 and have a sixty-four-year-old man open fire into a crowd at a Las Vegas concert, taking the lives of fifty-eight people. He didn't program a troubled teen in 2018 to kill fourteen students and three teachers at a high school in Parkland, Florida. He hates these things. He hates them more than we do.

Some may be thinking, "Hold on, God doesn't hate. He's a God of love." Then why does the Bible record so many things God hates? Proverbs 6:16-19 lists seven in just a few verses! Hate is the other side of the love coin. God hates what hurts the people He loves, which includes the atrocities people inflict on one another.

Sometimes in the aftermath of a horrible event I hear people say, "Well, it must have been God's will." That is so not true! God is not the author of evil and hates it (James 1:13). The devastation inflicted by terrorists on September 11, 2001, didn't happen by God's design. We need to understand that the very things that anger and break our hearts, anger and break the heart of God even more.

Then why do these things happen? If God is sovereign, isn't it all on Him? Isn't it His job to stop evil? Thoughts on this complex question fill many volumes, but let's look at it from a ten-thousand-foot level to see if we can get the big picture.

God's Choices

The world God created in the first two chapters of Genesis was just like heaven: perfect. But sin—the rebellion of people against God and His ways—changed all that and evil entered the playing field. This is something that is referred to as The Fall of Man. It was then that God made choices about how His broken world would work against the backdrop of His ultimate plan for redemption.

There's something important to understand about choices: every choice comes with a set of built-in limitations. If you choose to vacation at the beautiful beaches of Florida, you're limiting yourself to very flat terrain and won't be doing any mountain biking or downhill skiing. But you can do some great body surfing! If you go to an Italian restaurant for dinner, you can enjoy a tasty stromboli, but you're out of luck if you're in the mood for tacos or nachos. There are pluses and minuses to every choice.

This is what God did. In His sovereignty He made choices, and each of these resulted in both benefits and limitations.

Time and Space

One of His choices was that the world would operate in a framework of time and space. Heaven won't be like this, but earth is. This means everything has a life cycle bookended by a beginning and an end. The second law of thermodynamics—one of the foundational laws of science—tells us that everything in a closed system moves from a state of order to a state of disorder.

Yet even without science we know this to be true, because it's the story of our cars, garages, houses, clothes, and just about everything in our lives. Time doesn't make things better (OK, maybe wine) because the forces of rust, decay, rot, deterioration, and death are always at work. This can be very painful, especially when it does its work on our bodies and the bodies of those we love. But it's a reality that will never change this side of heaven.

The Byrds, one of America's iconic rock bands, released their second album with the title song *Turn, Turn, Turn*. The words come straight from Solomon in the opening verses of Ecclesiastes 3:

To everything, there is a season, and a time to every purpose under heaven. A time to be born, a time to die; a time to plant, a time to reap; a time to kill, a time to heal; a time to laugh, a time to cry; a time to build up, a time to break down; a time to dance, a time to mourn…

God's sovereign choice to frame the world in time and space means there will be a time to be born and a time to die. We celebrate the first but dread the second. We love the building, laughing, dancing, and healing, but the framework of time and space means it will eventually come to an end. It's all part of the old order: this is not heaven.

When the cartilage in my left hip wore thin and I began to walk with a painful limp, it wasn't because God was doing anything wrong. It simply meant that the created framework of time and space was working as it was supposed to.

Sometimes when I hear people complaining about the wearing out of things—especially if they haven't budgeted for it—I have to bite my tongue to keep from responding with a sarcastic, "Did you think your air conditioner came with forever parts, or your car was blessed with everlasting tires?" Everything on earth will eventually wear out; our cars, shoes, houses, and ultimately our bodies and hearts. This isn't because God is pushing the doom button to make our lives miserable. It's simply the way it was designed to work from the beginning. This is not heaven.

Reliable and Predictable Laws

Another of God's choices was that everything would run on a system of reliable and predictable laws. Just think how wonderful this is! When I turned on the shower this morning, the water didn't go up and soak the ceiling—but down! Wow, how amazing! And it's been doing it my whole life.

When I shot my basketball yesterday afternoon, guess what happened: it went down through the hoop (at least a few times). My car stayed on the road, my shirts hung down from the pole in the closet, and my shoes rested on the floor. All this happened because of the reliable and predictable laws of gravity and physics.

These laws also mean that the mixing of certain substances and chemicals will always yield the same results, which is the basis of research and science. It's because of reliable and predictable laws that the body's digestive, respiratory, nervous, muscular, lymphatic, endocrine, and cardiovascular systems work.

It's why there is evaporation, wind, fog, rain, and snow. It's why water freezes at thirty-two degrees and boils at two hundred twelve degrees Fahrenheit. Unless you're in Denver, where the reliable law of air pressure causes it to boil at two hundred two degrees, or in La Paz, Bolivia, at only one hundred ninety. It's because of these reliable and predictable laws that things work. Without them we would live in a perpetual state of turmoil and confusion.

But when heavy objects collide or fall from high elevations, these same laws of physics and gravity can cause great pain, destruction, and loss. While the force of moving water can turn turbines to generate electricity, it can also demolish homes and sweep cars from the road. The science of combining oxygen and heat to produce the benefits of fire can also destroy property and life. These reliable and predictable laws are all part of earth dwelling.

Freedom of Choice

This one is huge. God chose to give the living souls He created the freedom to choose because that's the only way they could love. It would take love for them to experience deep and meaningful relationships both with Him and one another. This is a big part of what it means to be created in His image because robots can't love. All they can do is repeat programmed words and obey commands without feelings or emotions. To love requires choice.

This was risky because it opened the possibility that God's beloved masterpieces would choose wrong. And sure enough, that's what they did. They abused their freedom and used it to reject God and His ways. They placed themselves at the center of His universe and treated it as if it were their own. They didn't trust Him and set up their own operating system of right and wrong, morality, relationships, and conflict resolution. They even created God in their own image, making

Him just like they wanted so they could call the shots and be in control.

But it didn't take long for things to unravel. Soon there were hundreds, then thousands, then millions and billions of people all writing their own stories that led to selfishness, greed, hatred, revenge, and prejudice. The incredible freedom of choice that God had given people, making it possible for them to give and receive love, got abused. And it affected everyone.

One of my sons and I spent weeks working on his bicycle when he was in middle school. We took it apart, cleaned every piece, replaced parts, put it back together, and then painted it the perfect color. It looked good and we were downright proud! But a few months later it was stolen right out of our garage. That wasn't God. That was someone abusing their freedom of choice to satisfy their selfish desires at our expense. God hated it, and so did I.

When Joy was robbed at gunpoint early in our marriage, that wasn't God. That was someone caring more about themselves than her.

When my car was stolen from my office and used to smash into an electronics store in a robbery, that wasn't God. It was people driven by greed, and I paid the price.

When a car crashed into the back of our house, destroying both my study and guitar, that wasn't God. Two students chose to break the law, and their choice affected me.

Every day we and those around us make choices that cause inconvenience, pain, grief, loss, and even death. It's how things work in the old order: this is not heaven.

New Life in the Old Order

So is that it? Do we just have to take a deep breath, think happy thoughts, and count down the days until we get to leave the old order and check into the new? Well, yes and no. Let's start with the yes.

The old order is never going to change this side of heaven, and God is not going to stop evil. It's not His job. Evil didn't exist in His original creation, and even after The Fall, He fashioned a behavioral system that would keep it under control. But people didn't want God's involvement and came up with their own plan. Evil is simply the consequence of the human choice to reject God and His ways. One day He will bring it to an end, but that day is not today. This is not heaven.

In the meantime, our experiences will continue to be framed by time and space, reliable and predictable laws, and the choices we and others make. God never intended for earth dwelling to provide what only heaven can. If we think it should, we'll end up very unhappy campers.

But couldn't He at least throw down some cosmic trump card every now and then and change the way the world works? Sure, He could. That's what miracles are: God stepping in and overruling the natural order.

I've experienced it and you may have too. And I love it! There's nothing like seeing God change the natural order in a way that makes you and others sit up and go, "Wow, thank you, God!"

But here's something to think about: Why should He? Why should He choose to overrule the natural order? That's a tricky question, isn't it? If we're honest, the primary reason is because we want our lives to be easier, less painful, and more enjoyable. We want God to make earth dwelling more like heaven, but that's not His agenda and He won't do it. He won't exempt us from the human experience of being earth-dwellers. Earth will always be earth, and if it weren't, we might not want to leave it behind.

The miracles of Jesus recorded in the New Testament always seemed to have a bigger purpose than just making life a little more comfortable for a short time. Sick people made well still died, and those given food were hungry again the next day. Thousands never got any help at all. The miracles, more than anything, demonstrated Jesus' divinity in a way that drew people to Him. So if you want to see a miracle, keep that in mind.

But there is also a NO aspect to the earlier question. While God is not going to change the old order of this earth—or stop evil—He never intended for us to navigate its challenges on our own. It's way too hard.

American Express ran an advertising campaign some years back that highlighted situations calling for quick, convenient money, then throwing down an American Express card and saying, "Don't leave home without it."

Jesus is saying, "Don't leave home without Me. Don't try to navigate the good, the bad, and the ugly of this chaotic world on your own. I never designed you for that. I'm not going to change the way the world works because this is not heaven. But if you trust Me, I'll walk with you through every minefield, decay, loss, perplexity, and hurt. It won't always be pretty, it won't always make sense, and it won't always be painless. But I'll be there to hold you up when you feel the weight of the old order is about to take you under. I'll be there to heal your wounded heart and breathe life into your weary soul. You may carry scars, but I'll get you back on your feet so you can engage in the story I have for you. My presence will shine like a light in the darkness, bringing hope from the grave."

This is what moved the writer of Psalm 73 from his state of discouragement and despair to one of peace and expectancy:

> *When my heart was embittered and I was pierced within, then I was senseless and ignorant; I was like a beast before You. Nevertheless I am continually with You; You have taken hold of my right hand. With your counsel You will guide me…as for me, the nearness of God is my good; I have made the Lord GOD my refuge…*
>
> Psalm 73:21-24, 28

There was a man in the Old Testament who knew well the pains of the old order. He experienced the agony of betrayal by family and friends, the unfairness of being wrongly accused, and the consequences of bad choices made by both himself and others. Yet through it all, King David was able to write these memorable words:

> *Even though I walk through the darkest valley, I will fear no evil, for You are with me.*
>
> Psalm 23:4

When God called Abraham to uproot his family and move to an unknown land to be the father of a new nation, He never told him He'd change the rules of earth dwelling to make his life easier. And He didn't. His life is a story of wandering, hardship, betrayal, family pain, and uncertainty. But he got the one promise he needed as an earth dweller: *I will be with you.* It was on the stained parchment of the old order that He experienced God and his story was written. And when his earth dwelling days were over, he left the old behind and entered the new.

When God called Moses to lead the people of Israel from Egypt to Canaan, He never promised to alter the ways of earth to make his life easier. And He didn't. He experienced fear, loneliness, perplexity, loss, betrayal, and all the realities of his fellow earth-dwellers. But through it all, God gave him the only promise he needed: *I will be with you.* He, too, had his part in God's story written on the stained parchment of the old order. And when his earth dwelling days were over, he left the old behind and entered the new.

One day the earth dwelling part of the journey will come to an end for all of us. And when it does, every follower of Jesus will be introduced to the new order of heaven. Every tear will be wiped from their eyes, and never again will there be death or mourning or pain. Wrongs will be righted and scores settled because the old order will be gone forever.

As I was breathing in the anesthesia to put me under for my cancer surgery a dozen years ago, the last thing I remember thinking was: "Wonder if I wake up in heaven? Wow, that would be the best because I'd never again have to experience the pain and limitations of earth. All that would be gone forever. Heaven, here I come!"

Well, when I opened my eyes I was still an earth-dweller. I was still going to have to face another day of the old order's imperfections, challenges, and pains. I was still going to have to deal with broken cars, broken houses, and broken people. My body would continue to wear out and be in need of repair.

But I'd never have to face any of this alone, because I awoke to experience another day of the companionship and comfort of my loving Father in a world of chaos. And I awoke to another day of seeing how God would write my part in His story on the stained parchment of the old order.

Then one day it will really happen. One day I will shed the old and enter the new. And on that day, I'll never again have to say the words I've had to say for so many years: This is not heaven.

Because it will be. Forever.

Is it just the hope of having
peace and gladness by and by?
Though on earth are sighs and sorrows,
all is glorious in the sky?

No! the hope I have now gives me
joy and peace beyond compare,
And my blessed Lord has taken,
all my trials and my care.

No, we need not cross the river
ere our dark forebodings cease;
For just now my heart's o'erflowing
with a stream of perfect peace.

Georgia C. Elliott

Chapter Five

GOD REALLY LOVES THE WORLD

Most people have a hard time believing God—or anyone else for that matter—really loves them. Our interactions with others confirm the suspicion that love is conditional, has to be earned, and can be lost if performance drops below expectations. No one gets married planning for things to unravel as they parrot the words, "For better or worse." But when reality hits and their version of worse actually happens, those ideals quickly vanish. Unconditional love is not a human characteristic.

Then somewhere along the way you hear about a God who loves differently. Not a "because of" love, but "in spite of." This is hard to understand because, even in the world of religion, there are things you have to DO to EARN your acceptance from whatever deity you're playing to. Then, when you mess up, you OWE in the form of penance to EARN your way back up the ladder. It's all very conditional and exhausting—earn and owe, earn and owe—but makes perfect sense from a human perspective.

But what we find in Jesus is something very different. Instead of making us earn His acceptance and love, He *earned it for us* by paying what we owed. This sounds too good to be true because it's counter to our human experience, but these words from the New Testament tell the story:

> *For while we were still helpless, at the right time Christ died for the ungodly...God demonstrates His own love toward us, in that while we were still sinners, Christ died for us.*
>
> Romans 5:6, 8

He didn't love us *after* we'd cleaned up our act or *after* we'd promised never to mess up again. No, but *while we were still sinners* is when God stepped in. No more EARN and OWE!

But there's more. The Apostle Paul tells us something in 2 Corinthians 5:21 that's so far beyond our comprehension it's hard to even imagine:

> *He made Him who knew no sin to be sin on our behalf,* **so that we might become the righteousness of God in Him.**

Did you get that? From the moment we enter into what Jesus has done for us, we're seen by God as being as righteous as He is. Not because of anything we've done, but because of what Jesus accomplished at the cross.

> *For He has clothed me with garments of salvation, He has wrapped me with a robe of righteousness…*
>
> Isaiah 61:10

No *earning* of His love, and no *owing* to appease Him when we fail. He's wrapped us in *His righteousness* so we can experience the joy of His life and love every day of our lives. This sounds almost blasphemous, but it's the beautiful story of the grace of God who really loves us.

Once we've received His wonderful gift and begin to live in a relationship with God, John 3:16 becomes very personal. Instead of reading, "God so loved the world that He gave His one and only Son…", we insert our own names: "God so loved ME…God so loved RON." It's not just the world He loves but me, which is so personal and meaningful.

Sometimes when I'm trying to help someone grasp the magnitude of what Jesus has done for them, I'll insert their name into the verse: "God so loved Larry that He gave His one and only Son. It's not just the world, Larry, but you. That's how much He loves you."

As we continue to grow in our faith, there may again be times we find ourselves doubting God's love, especially when we've gone off the rails and experienced failure. But these become fewer and fewer as we learn to live in the confidence of His everlasting love and forgiveness. We KNOW we are right with Him and look forward to the day we get to move from the old order to our permanent location. So what are we to do in the meantime? Live like pigs in mud as we roll around in the blessings of God?

Divinity in Humanity

Here's something I've learned in following Jesus that has become a significant thread in the fabric of my life. As wonderful as it is to live in the love and friendship of Jesus—and it IS wonderful—that's not why we're still hanging around this planet. God has a part for us earth-dwellers in His story today, tomorrow, and every day until we relocate.

When those God had created chose to trust themselves instead of Him and chart their own course, it broke His heart. So, as we've seen, He set in motion a plan to fix the problem and redeem the people He loves back into a relationship with Him. Much of the Old Testament chronicles the unfolding of this plan: Abraham, Moses, David, Elijah, Daniel, and the nation of Israel all playing critical roles in a redemptive plan that was headed somewhere.

Then, two thousand years ago, God so loved the world that He gave His Son to put an exclamation point on the plan: "It is finished!" (John 19:30). These final words of Jesus from the cross declared that the redemptive plan was now complete through His death. It's done, and if you've crossed that line of faith you're good. It is finished.

But there's a question that begs to be answered: Does God still love the world as much today as He did 2000 years ago? There's a good chance most of us would answer that in the affirmative. If so, then what's His plan for distributing that love to the billions of people scattered across our planet? He had a redemptive plan that brought Jesus from heaven to earth for thirty-three years and culminated at the cross. But what about today?

When John introduces Jesus in the first chapter of the gospel that bears his name, here's what he says:

No one has ever seen God, but the one and only Son, who is Himself God and is in closest relationship with the Father, has made Him known.
John 1:18 NIV

No one had ever seen God. But watching Jesus in real time cleared up many of their misconceptions and gave them a clearer understanding of who He was. It was divinity living in humanity—flesh and blood—that made the difference. People could *see* the truth and love of God like never before and were drawn to Him.

But Jesus is gone. That human life that made God known to the people He loved is no longer here. Or is it?

Jesus told His disciples something on His final night that was to change their lives. Although He was leaving, He would be sending a replacement who would be *with them* and *in them* forever: the Holy Spirit (John 14:16-26). And it was to be the same for every follower of Jesus from then on (Romans 8:9). Said another way, from that time on every follower of Jesus would have His divinity living in their humanity.

God set a plan in motion that was every bit as intentional as the plan He'd orchestrated throughout the pages of the Old Testament. While He wants His followers to live in the deep joy of His love and companionship, there's more. *Our humanity, just like Jesus', is to be the vehicle for distributing the reality of God to the world.* If we fail to do this and make it only about ourselves, we end up creating a very me-centered, narcissistic Christianity; a very selfish John 3:16. It's OK to start there. In fact, it *has* to start there. But it's never to stay there.

We've got to put the WORLD back into John 3:16

Conduits of Blessing

It's surprising how many times in the New Testament we find the little phrase "so that" connected to God's blessing of our lives. This is letting us know that God blesses us not only for our own benefit, but *so that* we can be conduits—channels through which something flows—of His blessing and love to the world. It's the story of what happens when divinity lives in humanity. This is one of the critical threads I've worked hard to weave into the fabric of my life over the years, and it's changed the way I look at our chaotic world.

The New Testament book of 2 Corinthians contains a number of these *so thats*. Here's one that sets the stage for all the rest:

> *The love of Christ controls us, having concluded this, that one died for all, therefore all died…*
>
> 2 Corinthians 5:14

This tells us that being controlled by the love of Christ is the foundation for everything Paul is about to say. Understanding His love is the force that drives us to think and act differently. He continues:

> *And He died for all, **so that**…*
>
> 2 Corinthians 5:15

How would you complete that sentence? *So that* we can be forgiven of our sins? *So that* we can spend eternity in heaven? *So that* we can have God's ear when life hits the fan? All of these are great truths, but let's keep reading:

> *He died for all, **so that** those who live might no longer live for themselves but for Him who died and rose on their behalf.*

Wow!! He died to free us from the tyranny of ourselves! He died to free us from living in a way that depletes our souls, damages our relationships, and leaves us empty. He died to free us from a me-centered life *so that* we can live a God-centered life of giving, serving, and loving the world He loves. He died to give us a life that is so much bigger, so much more meaningful, and so much more fulfilling.

Resistance

But our default settings resist this. It won't work. If we don't look out for number one, nobody else will and we'll lose. Knowing our natural bent toward self-preservation, God makes a deal with us:

> *But seek first His kingdom and His righteousness, and all these things will be added to you.*
>
> Matthew 6:33

This statement concludes a section of the Sermon on the Mount where Jesus is warning His listeners to not let fear and anxiety turn them into self-consumed worriers. He then offers them the deal of a lifetime that goes something like this: "You've already trusted Me for your eternity; now I want you to trust Me for what happens between now and heaven. If you'll let Me love and bless the world through you, I promise to have your back and take care of the things you're worried about. We good?" When we agree to His deal, we find ourselves stepping into a whole new kind of freedom. But we can't do that until we understand and embrace how much God loves us.

I find it interesting that many we find ourselves venerating are ones who've made this deal. I can't help but think of Mother Teresa, a woman who was committed to letting her little five-foot body be a conduit for delivering the love and goodness of God to the poorest of the poor in India. She was awarded the Nobel Peace Prize in 1979. God so loved the world that He gave it Mother Teresa for eighty-seven years, and He had her back every step of the way.

God Never Wastes an Experience

Here's another *so that* in 2 Corinthians. Paul lets those he's writing know that he and his team had experienced fierce opposition. They'd been robbed, whipped, and beaten in their travels. Here's what he writes in the opening paragraph of his letter:

> *Praise be to the God and Father of our Lord Jesus Christ, the Father of compassion and the God of all comfort, who comforts us in all our troubles…*
>
> 2 Corinthians 1:3-4 NIV

Don't you just love it when the comfort of God rushes in to breathe life into your hurting soul? I've experienced it many times, and it's what keeps me going when I feel like I'm down for the count. Thank you, Jesus! But Paul doesn't stop there:

> ...*who comforts us in all our troubles **so that** we can comfort those in any trouble with the comfort we ourselves receive from God.*

Was God's *only* interest in comforting Paul to make his earth dwelling days a little easier and less painful? No. The old order of this world will dish out a lot of pain, and none of us is exempt. But God never wastes an experience. He loves the world so much that He comforts us in our hurting times *so that* we can be conduits of that same love and comfort to others. It's the reality of divinity living through our humanity.

Money on the Move

One more out of 2 Corinthians. Paul had written the churches in Greece to see if any of them could help those being affected by famine in Israel. The Corinthian church had said they would, so he lets them know in his letter that he'll be there soon to pick up their contribution. And being the teacher he is, he uses the opportunity to remind them of the ways of God when it comes to money. This is found in chapters eight and nine.

He starts by reminding them they should never give out of pressure or guilt, but cheerfully. Then, knowing that most of them didn't have much, he tells them this:

God is able to bless you abundantly…

2 Corinthians 9:8 NIV

It's clear from the context of the chapter that he's not talking about some general kind of blessing but money. Sounds a little self-serving, doesn't it? Give to get more! But hang on. Why was God going to bless them with additional resources? So they could get a new camel, more fashionable sandals, or upgraded wagon wheels? Nothing wrong with any of these, but it's not what he's talking about here:

*And God is able to bless you abundantly, **so that** in all things at all times, having all that you need, you will abound in every good work.*

He's saying God is going to increase their supply of money so it can flow through them in doing good for the people and things He loves. And just in case we're a little slow, he spells it out even clearer in the next few verses:

*Now He who supplies seed to the sower and bread for food will also supply and increase your store of seed and will enlarge the harvest of your righteousness. You will be enriched in every way **so that** you can be generous on every occasion, and through us, your generosity will result in thanksgiving to God.*

2 Corinthians 9:10-12 NIV

God loves the world so much that He's going to resource us financially, not only to meet our own needs, but so it can flow *through us* in a way that brings thanksgiving to God.

Joy and I have made it a habit for many years to not automatically assume unexpected or additional resources we receive are for us. Have we been entrusted with them so they can be moved someplace else? Are we just the conduits? Sometimes the answer is yes, and other times no. It's never a guilt thing but simply a response to knowing that God wants to love and bless the world through us.

Masterpiece Wiring

Let's take another look at Ephesians 2:8-10 from the perspective of God's loving of the world:

> *God saved you by His grace when you believed. And you can't take credit for this; it is a gift from God. Salvation is not a reward for the good things we have done, so none of us can boast about it. For we are God's masterpiece. He has created us anew in Christ Jesus…*

Paul starts by reminding us that all the credit for our salvation belongs to God. He is the one who loved us and gave His life to redeem ours. There is no room for boasting: all the credit goes to Him. Understanding this should reduce us to a puddle of gratitude.

Then He calls us His masterpiece. That's quite a compliment coming from the living God! He created each of us with a uniqueness that is unlike anyone on the planet. Maybe He made you super smart with an IQ that's off the charts. Maybe He made you musical, artsy, crafty, mechanical, good with numbers, good with your hands, or an organizational guru. Maybe He gave you an infectious personality, an analytical mind for complex problem-solving, or the ability to turn anything you touch into gold. There's no right or wrong or better or worse in any of this: it's all the handiwork of our loving God.

But have you ever stopped to ask yourself why? Why did He make you the way He did? Most of us try to use our unique wiring in choosing our vocations, which is good. Yet these verses tell us we've been created *anew* because of the cross of Jesus. What is that all about? The answer is found in the *"so that"* at the end of verse 10:

> *For we are God's masterpiece. He has created us anew in Christ Jesus **so that** we can do the good things He planned for us long ago.*

Think about that for a moment. God uniquely hard-wired each of us from the very beginning to play the part He had for us in His story of loving and redeeming the world. We couldn't step into that until we had a relationship with Him, but once we did, our masterpiece status changed from inactive to active. And what do active masterpieces do? They join God in His story by using their God-given masterpiece wiring and design.

For years I used my masterpiece wiring of creativity, leadership, and entrepreneurship to make money and entertain through the creative arts and business. But I've also used them to start churches and creatively draw people to the love and ways of Jesus. Some with organizational skills have used them to advance relief efforts, others good with their hands to build beds for under-resourced children, and still others with financial proficiencies to fund ministries in moving the message of Jesus across the world. The possibilities are endless. It's the only reasonable response when the love of God controls us.

God loves the world so much that He has uniquely wired each of us as His masterpiece to be conduits of His love. Jesus may be gone physically, but His divinity is still very present in our humanity.

Purpose Driven Living

There are dozens of these *so that's* throughout the Scriptures, but let me close with one more. It comes from the last chapter of Paul's final letter before his execution.

> *At my first defense, no one supported me, but all deserted me. May it not be counted against them.*
>
> 2 Timothy 4:16

Paul had been imprisoned in Rome for his preaching of the gospel, and not a single person had supported him at his trial. Today he is revered for moving the message of Jesus across the known world, but not back then; he was alone. Then we read this remarkable statement:

But the Lord stood with me and strengthened me…

verse 17

God was right there with him in his time of greatest need. When everyone had deserted Him, God had not. Why? The most obvious and correct answer is because that's exactly what He'd promised to do.

But let's take this one step further. Maybe the bigger question is, why was God even keeping Paul alive? If he died he'd be in the presence of Jesus and no longer have to suffer the discomfort and abuse of living in a dark prison. Let's keep reading:

But the Lord stood with me and strengthened me **so that** *through me the proclamation might be fully accomplished and all the Gentiles might hear, and I was rescued out of the lion's mouth.*

God didn't keep Paul alive just so he could play one more round of golf, watch one more Super Bowl, or finally get to check that Mediterranean cruise off his bucket list. God loved the world so much that He was going to keep Paul alive a little longer *so that* more people could hear the good news and experience a forever relationship with the living God.

Most of us want to live long lives, but have you ever asked yourself why? After all, in heaven there'll be no taxes or political unrest, no broken cars or broken houses, and no broken bodies.

The Apostle Paul was done with earth dwelling and was ready to get his ticket punched for heaven. He was good to go. But God still had a part for Him in His story, so He chose to inconvenience him by extending his life.

Intentional Inconvenience

I've learned in my years of walking with Jesus that He will sometimes interrupt my plans because there's someone He wants to love through me. I know this sounds a bit inconsiderate of God because, after all, we have lives, right? But when we stop to think about what it actually means to be a follower of Jesus— well, I think you get the idea. Followers don't lead; they follow. And that following can sometimes be inconvenient when it messes with our plans.

Several months ago one of my sons was having new carpet put in his house. A date was set for the installation and I volunteered to supervise the project since he would be at work. But things fell apart the day before it was to happen. The installers picked up the wrong carpet and, because of the lost time, wouldn't be able to do the job until the following week. That wouldn't work for us, so we made dozens of calls to line up someone else, but no one could do it on such short notice. Very frustrating and very inconvenient!

Then I did something I've trained myself to do over the years. I simply said, "OK God, what are You up to? Am I missing something?" We finally connected with an installer, and I was there to meet him the following morning when he arrived. We began chatting as he rolled out the carpet padding on the garage floor, and before I knew it, he was telling me the sad story of his life. So I took a Sharpie and, there on the carpet padding, sketched a simple explanation of the good news of God's redemption through the cross. He asked a few questions and then, standing there in the garage, he stepped into a relationship with Jesus. God so loved the world that He inconvenienced me *so that* His love could be communicated to a life that was changed.

We began this chapter talking about how important it is to take the *world* out of John 3:16 and put in our own names. This is a critical first step because understanding God's love for us is what drives everything. But then we saw that leaving the verse that way can lead to a very me-centered, narcissistic Christianity. We've got to put the world back into John 3:16.

But once we've done that, we need to again put our names in the verse—but in a different place:

God loves the world so much that He gave it ME to be a conduit of His love and grace.

- God loves the world so much that He delivers me from a selfish life *so that* He can love others through me.

- God loves the world so much that He comforts me when I'm hurting *so that* I can comfort others.

- God loves the world so much that He resources me financially *so that* I can help resource those He loves.

- God loves the world so much that He inconveniences me *so that* His life-giving message can be given to others.

These are not things we do to *earn* God's love, but things we do because He *already* loves us. His heart becomes our heart, and we find ourselves living and loving like Jesus.

Over the years I've developed the habit of beginning nearly every day with this simple prayer: "Thanks for giving me another day that You've made. I don't know exactly what You're up to, but I know it involves loving people. So I'm signing up to be used by You today in any way You choose. Help me to be sensitive to what You're up to so I'll say and do the right thing when the opportunity arises."

I'm sure I've missed plenty of these, but I've also had the joy of connecting with a lot of them. And when I do, I find myself saying—sometimes right out loud—"I was born for this. Thank You, God, for using my humanity as a conduit of who You are to the people You love. Thank you for including me in Your story."

And it just doesn't get any better than that!

Out in the highways and byways of life,
many are weary and sad;
Carry the sunshine where darkness is rife,
making the sorrowing glad.

Give as was given to you in your need,
love as the Master loved you;
Be to the helpless a helper indeed,
unto your mission be true.

Make me a blessing, make me a blessing,
out of my life may Jesus shine;
Make me a blessing, O Savior I pray,
make me a blessing to someone today.

Ira B. Wilson

Chapter Six

JOINING THE
MOVEMENT OF GOD

There is one more *so that* I had planned to include in the last chapter, but it is so central that I decided it needed a chapter of its own. Weaving a life of purpose in our changing world has everything to do with being part of something that is so much bigger than any of us and will be around long after we're gone. This *something* plays a huge part in the story God is writing and includes every person who is a follower of Jesus.

The Apostle Peter wrote two letters that are found near the end of the New Testament. He knew well the history of God's choosing of Israel as His people—a holy nation—to carry out the first phase of His redemptive plan for the world. The cross had brought that phase to an end and, within a few years of Jesus' death, Rome would erase Israel from the map.

But God's redemptive plan was far from over. The next phase would involve the raising of a new people—a new holy nation—to work with Him. Here is how Peter described it:

*But you are a chosen people, a royal priesthood, a holy nation, a people for God's own possession, **so that** you may proclaim the excellencies of Him who has called you out of darkness into His marvelous light; for you once were not a people, but now you are the people of God; you had not received mercy, but now you have received mercy.*

I Peter 2:9-10

This *new nation* was not to be defined by geographical boundaries or cultural ethnicities: It was the inclusive gathering of all followers of Jesus. They were now the chosen of God—the holy nation—who were to play a critical role in the next phase of God's redemptive plan for the world. And this new *nation* had a name: the church.

Now I'm sure everyone has an opinion of the church that comes from participation, observation, or both. For some it represents a place of friendship and community, while for others a place of criticism and condemnation. Some see it as fertile soil for developing a growing relationship with God, while for others it represents a distortion of God that is ugly and distasteful. For some it helps to connect the layered dimensions of life, while for others it's confusing and disconnected from the real world. Yet the church is not a human idea, but God's. And when we see it through His eyes—which can be challenging in our culture— we discover it to be much different than many of us have ever imagined or experienced.

Nearly five decades ago, I had what today I call *the twenty-four hours that changed my life*. Next to coming into a relationship with Jesus and getting married, that single day had the greatest impact on my future. I was flying from California to Florida in January of 1973 to evaluate and update a traveling theatrical production. There was a man I'd met several years earlier I wanted to visit on the way, so I arranged for a one-day stop in Houston, Texas.

He picked me up at the airport and we drove to his home for breakfast, where I filled him in on what I'd been up to since we'd last spoken. After I'd finished giving him the high points of my *very* impressive life, he asked, "Do you mind if I share a few things with you?" And so it began.

Soon his wife was serving us lunch at the table we'd never moved from, and then dinner. The hours flew by as he opened the Scriptures and, for the first time, I began to see how the church was God's master plan for keeping all Jesus had started moving across the world. What I learned in those hours has been a strong thread in the fabric of my life ever since.

Let's think again about John 3:16 from one more perspective that is very much in line with the heart of God:

God loves the world so much that He gave it the church to be the delivery system of the fullness of Jesus.

I love the church. I've spent nearly thirty-five years of my life starting and leading churches. I love seeing life change. I love it when the church stands in the gap as the movement of God in bringing the love and truth of Jesus to a broken world. I love it when people grow in their faith and become a loving community of Jesus followers who are looking more like Him every day in His person and purpose. There's nothing like it.

But I don't love it when the church turns inward and becomes all about itself. I don't love it when the church turns into a Jesus Club of insiders with little thought or concern for those still on the outside. I don't love it when the church becomes a me-centered, narcissistic experience that forgets about its redemptive place in the plan of God. I don't love it when the church stops being for the world. I don't love it when the church stops being the church.

I don't think any of this ever happens intentionally. Most churches start with a desire to see people come into a relationship with Jesus and then grow in their faith. But over time, the focus gradually shifts and becomes all about taking care of those inside the walls. "We need more stuff for US. What is there for the kids and the teens? What about something for the women, and let's not forget the men. We need more Bible studies and small groups and times of 'fellowship.'" Then there's the endless push for volunteers to step up and "serve" to keep all the machinery running. Before long it becomes a church of insiders doing insider things while the outsiders, quite literally, are left in the dark.

The Body of Christ

The most common imagery used in the New Testament for the church is the Body of Christ.

> *And God placed all things under His feet and appointed Him* (Jesus) *to be head over everything for the church, which is His body, the fullness of Him who fills everything in every way.*
>
> Ephesians 1:22-23 NIV

There was a time when God had a physical body on this planet, and His name was Jesus. As we saw in the last chapter, He lived with the heart and purpose of His Father in a way that gave people a clearer understanding of God. He stood as a beacon of life and truth against a backdrop of ritual and dogma, and lives were changed forever. But that body was only on the earth for a short time. Yet, in His wisdom, *God replaced His single body with a collective body called the church.* The heart and purpose of God hadn't changed one bit; only the form.

If we were to use the literal body of Jesus as the template for the church and follow Him around for a few days, what do you think we'd find? What would He spend His time doing? Let me suggest that everything He did—the fullness of Jesus—can be summed up in three words: Redemption, Restoration, and Distribution. Let's take a brief look at each of these. I'm going to spend more time on the first because it's the one that usually gets overlooked and neglected.

REDEMPTION
An Outward Focused Movement

The first time the church is mentioned in the New Testament is in a conversation Jesus was having with Peter:

> ...*I will build My church, and the gates of Hades will not overpower it.*
>
> Matthew 16:18

As noble as this sounds, I don't think Peter had a clue what Jesus was talking about. His thoughts were of an earthly kingdom where he and the others would share leading roles. But Jesus had something very different in mind: a new movement that would be known as the church. Not a location or building, but the community of all His followers carrying His truth, life, and love to every corner of the earth. And *redemption* was at the core of everything:

- at the incarnation: "You shall call His name Jesus, for He will save His people from their sins." (Luke 1:21)
- at the calling of His first followers: "Follow Me, and I will make you become fishers of men." (Mark 1:17)
- to dishonest Zaccheus, after having lunch with Jesus: "The Son of Man has come to seek and to save that which was lost." (Luke 19:10)

- in response to the Pharisee's criticism of His spending time with the wrong kinds of people: "I did not come to call the righteous, but sinners to repentance." (Luke 5:30-32)
- to the disciple's questions about signs of the end times: "The gospel must first be preached to all the nations." (Mark 13:10)

Any who spent time with Jesus had no question that redemption was at the very core of everything He did.

Jesus reminds His followers in the opening chapter of the Book of Acts that He is going to be giving them His Spirit—the Holy Spirit—for the task He's entrusting to them:

But you will receive power when the Holy Spirit has come on you; and you shall be My witnesses both in Jerusalem, and in all Judea and Samaria, and even to the remotest part of the earth.

Acts 1:8

The church has been about reaching those outside the walls from the very beginning. The starting bell sounded within a few days of Jesus saying this, all His followers received the Holy Spirit, and the very first thing they did with their new power was *talk about Jesus to those around them*. I wonder where they got that idea? Three thousand became followers of Jesus that day and the church—the movement of God—was born.

As the movement continued to move, more and more outsiders were becoming followers of Jesus. This created a problem for the Jewish officials, so they stepped in to slow things down. They hauled in Peter and John, the movement's leaders, and gave them strict orders to stop talking about Jesus with the outsiders. They could have their own little Jesus Club if they wanted to, but no more recruiting. Here is their response:

> *Whether it is right in the sight of God to listen to you rather than to God, make your own judgment; for we cannot stop speaking about what we have seen and heard.*
>
> Acts 4:19-20

The religious leaders were telling them to stop doing the very thing Jesus had told them to do. Who were they to listen to? They quickly conferred with their companions upon their release, and it was unanimous. "We've got to keep doing what Jesus told us: we've got to talk with the outsiders." We then read this:

> *And when they had prayed, the place where they had gathered together was shaken, and they were all filled with the Holy Spirit and began to speak the word of God with boldness.*
>
> Acts 4:31

This is now the third time the Holy Spirit is mentioned in the life of Jesus' followers, and each time it was for the same purpose: to empower them to get the good news of redemption to the outsiders. God loves the world so much that He gave it the church.

Passing the Baton

Soon all Jerusalem was buzzing with the chatter of Jesus, which led to the arrest of *all* the apostles. This time they are beaten and again told to stop talking about Jesus with the outsiders. But they don't, and more and more continue to come to faith in Christ.

Then God enlists a man by the name of Saul in a way only He can. Saul had been a leader in the opposition of this new movement and then became a follower of Jesus! His name is changed to Paul and God sends him across Asia Minor and Europe to let the outsiders know about the saving grace of Jesus. *He never went to a city to start a church but to tell people about God's way of redemption through the cross.* It was only when some became followers that a church would be born. Then, after spending time helping them understand more of the ways of Jesus, he'd pass the baton to them to keep the movement *moving* while he and his team went to another city. So did they get it? Did these new communities of Christ-followers pick it up and keep it moving?

Paul had gone to the city of Thessalonica in Greece, spoken with outsiders, and when some came to faith a church was started. But an uprising forced him and his friends to leave the city much earlier than they'd planned. Because of his concern for them, he sent his coworker, Timothy, back to Thessalonica to see how they were doing.

When Timothy returned with an encouraging report, Paul dashed off a letter to them that is today known as 1 Thessalonians. After a warm introduction, he writes:

> *You became imitators of us and of the Lord...you became a model to all the believers in Macedonia and Achaia. **The Lord's message rang out from you** not only in Macedonia and Achaia—your faith in God has become known everywhere. Therefore, we do not need to say anything about it.*
>
> 1 Thessalonians 1:6-8 NIV

They had gotten what Paul had told them! Although they didn't know much, they at least understood the church was never to be an insiders club and had moved the good news of Jesus to the surrounding areas. The movement moved because the church embraced its role in God's redemptive plan.

On his third missionary trip, Paul went to the city of Ephesus on the western coast of Turkey. Outsiders had become followers of Jesus, and he continued to meet with them every day for two years to help them grow in their faith. And guess what happened?

*This went on for two years **so that all who lived in Asia heard the word of the Lord**, both Jews and Greeks.*

Acts 19:10

What today is commonly referred to as *discipleship* didn't result in notebooks filled with great Bible verses, but in the redemptive message of Jesus spreading throughout Asia Minor! They understood the church was an outward focused movement—and kept it moving.

But like all movements, it gradually slowed down, and this often messy and disorganized movement of God got organized. It got buildings, a well-oiled leadership structure, programs, and highly developed how-to manuals. And little by little this dynamic, outwardly focused movement began to turn inward. The wagons were circled to keep the bad people out, and a kind of holy judgementalism set in that was downright creepy to those outside the walls.

Somewhere along the way, the church forgot its part in God's redemptive plan for the world. Somewhere along the way, they forgot what the fullness of the body of Jesus looked like. Somewhere along the way, it became a club of insiders who liked talking about Jesus but not loving like Him. Somehow it forgot that God so loved the world that He gave it the church. Today Turkey, once alive with the transforming power of Jesus, is only 0.2% Christian. Somewhere along the way, the church stopped being the Body of Christ.

RESTORATION
Becoming Like Jesus

Every person who comes into a relationship with Jesus starts broken. Their thinking is far from the ways of Jesus, and these patterns have messed with their lives and relationships. They need to be restored so they can step into their masterpiece status in His story between now and heaven.

Jesus spent much of His time working to reorient His followers to think and act like Him: to replace their ways with His, to think about people like He did, and to be led by truth rather than feelings and impulses. And when He left, He passed this reorienting process on to His new body: the church.

In his first letter to his friend Timothy, Paul reminds him that the church is the "pillar and support of the truth" (I Timothy 3:15). Getting this truth rooted in the minds of those who follow Jesus is the cornerstone of restoration. It's not the responsibility of government or education to do this: it belongs to the church. And if the church doesn't do it, it won't get done. Paul reminds us of just how important this is in his letter to the church in Rome:

> *Do not be conformed to this world, but be transformed by the renewing of your mind, **so that** you may prove what God's will is, that which is good and acceptable and perfect.*
>
> Romans 12:2

God entrusts gifted men and women to the church to work with Him in this transformation process of mind renewal through the teaching of the Scriptures. Their God-given responsibility is not to give entertaining and clever Jesus talks, but to lay out the ways of God so people's minds and lives can be renewed. Only then will followers of Jesus be able to step into the part God has for them in His story.

A big part of this renewal is moving from an all-about-me, self-centered orientation to one that loves and worships God above anything else. As our understanding of His incredible love continues to seep deeper into our souls, it brings us to our knees and we find ourselves echoing the cry of Revelation 4:8, "Holy, Holy, Holy, is the Lord God, Almighty."

Another huge piece of the restoration process is experiencing the love and joy of being in community with other followers of Jesus. This provides the protection, encouragement, and support for stepping into the new story God has for each of them. When the waters run fast and deep, the community is there to lock arms and keep anyone from being pulled under.

This community also provides the context for using the spiritual gifts God entrusts to each of His followers. The literal body of Christ had *everything* because He was God in the flesh, but the new body of Christ is collective. This means no one person is a reflection of the fullness of Jesus on their own. Every person provides a piece—a part of the body— so together it can look and function like Jesus in the world He loves. A person's spiritual gifts can only be experienced to their fullest in the community of other Christ-followers.

But we must never forget that this restoration process has a purpose! It's not just to make life more enjoyable, although it will. It's not just to provide us with good friends and nice kids for our children to play with, although it will. It's not to turn earth into heaven, although it will certainly give us a taste. It's so we can grow up and join God in His redemptive story: *God loves the world so much that He gave it the church.*

DISTRIBUTION
The Divine Supply Chain

This brings us full circle. One of the things we'd find by following the physical body of Jesus for a few days is that He was always distributing something. To those with physical needs, He distributed food and healing. To the marginalized and forgotten, He distributed value and hope. To those thirsting for the reality of God, He distributed Himself. When Peter was trying to help a group of outsiders get a better understanding of Jesus, here's what he told them:

> *You know of Jesus of Nazareth, how God anointed Him with the Holy Spirit and with power, and how He went about doing good and healing all who were oppressed by the devil, for God was with Him.*
> Acts 10:38

I love that description! Jesus went around doing good and distributing good in its various forms. And His new body—the church—is to do the same. Redeemed and restored people begin to see themselves and those around them differently. When they work together as the collective body of Christ, they become a powerful movement to distribute His goodness and love to their community and world.

This is the WHAT of the church. The HOW can be as varied as leadership, geographical location, gifting, and time in history. It can gather in buildings, homes, outdoors, or in coffee shops. But when the WHAT gets lost in the HOW, or the WHAT of personal agendas replaces the heart and purpose of God, the church stops being the church and the world He loves loses.

Movements Advance

When Jesus first mentioned the church to Peter, He told him, "the gates of Hades will not overpower it." Think about what He's saying here: gates are for keeping things out and defending against advances. Jesus is saying that the adversary will not be able to stop the *advance* of the church. It was designed from the very beginning to be a movement that moves.

The classic World War II movie about General George Patton opens with a speech he's giving to a group of recruits. After a somewhat colorful introduction—calling them sons of something other than their mothers—he says, "I don't want to get any messages saying that we are holding our position. We're not holding anything…we are advancing constantly, and we're not interested in holding on to anything except the enemy…."

I can hear Jesus saying that: "I don't want to get any messages saying that the church is holding its position and defending the faith. We're not holding or defending anything: we're advancing. We're taking the light of the gospel into the darkness because the church is the fullness of Jesus, bringing redemption to the world."

Advancing has always been a top-shelf priority of the churches I've had the joy of starting and leading over the years. When we went to College Station, Texas, we brought in nearly a hundred people for several weeks to do nothing but meet outsiders and share the gospel of Jesus Christ. When a number of outsiders experienced the redemptive power of Jesus, the church was born. That value has remained a priority to this day.

When I was involved in starting a church in Central Florida, a student ministry was launched to reach outsiders in the high schools. Once they came into a relationship with Jesus, we then focused on seeing their parents experience the same. We had no intention of holding our position but of advancing, and hundreds came to know the life-changing love of Jesus.

My primary reason for becoming a pastor was to join the redemptive movement of God through the local church, and it's been a thrill I'll cherish forever. Yet the most difficult challenge I faced year after year was keeping the value of redemption white hot. Followers of Jesus find it easier to drift toward restoration kinds of programming because it benefits them directly. It's a non-threatening insider thing they can enjoy with their friends and family, and life is good.

Sheep Imagery

Jesus is called the *good shepherd* in the New Testament, and His followers are referred to as *sheep*. Churches are spoken of as *flocks,* and those who care for them are called *shepherds* (pastors, elders). The sheep imagery helps us to see that the church is to be a well-cared-for, healthy flock of Jesus followers.

So here's a question: how can you tell if a flock of four-legged woolly sheep is healthy? One of the surest signs is reproduction. If they are well cared for, a ewe (female sheep) will give birth to one to three lambs a year. It's natural and expected because that's what happens when sheep are healthy and growing. Something is wrong if it's not.

What does a flock of healthy and growing two-legged spiritual sheep look like? What are the signs? I hear the word *discipleship* tossed around a lot, but it's important to understand that discipleship is about helping people *become like Jesus in both His person and purpose*. We're told in Luke 6:40 that when disciples are fully trained they'll be like their teacher.

It's hard to imagine anyone becoming like Jesus without having His heart for redemption at the very core of their being. It should be natural and expected that any healthy and growing follower of Jesus reproduces.

Yet most discipleship today has very little—if anything—to do with practically envisioning and helping followers to be like Jesus in His heart for reaching outsiders. It just doesn't sell well and lacks the buzz that draws the insiders.

God loves the world so much that He gave it the church, His body, to look, live, and love like Him as it continues everything He started.

And God placed all things under His feet and appointed Him (Jesus) *to be head over everything for the church, which is His body,* **the fullness of Him who fills everything in every way.**
Ephesians 1:22-23 NIV

When outsiders look at the church, they should find themselves drawn to irresistible people who are reflections of the irresistible Jesus.

When they experience the power of redemption, they should find themselves drawn into a loving community of restoration where they are taught and cared for as they grow into the masterpieces God designed them to be.

As they continue to become more like Jesus, they should find themselves on the distribution side of the supply chain because it's no longer just about them, but the world.

God loves the world so much that He gave it the church to be the delivery system of the fullness of Jesus. And when we're part of His enduring movement—a purpose-driven loving community that is so much bigger than any of us and will be around long after we're gone—we can't help but live with a deep sense of destiny and purpose.

REDEMPTION • RESTORATION • DISTRIBUTION

The church is not a people-driven movement or a stage for the promotion of gifted and charismatic leaders. It is the living, grass-roots movement of God to bring His love, life, and transforming power to the world of people He died to redeem.

Chapter Seven

THE BIBLE DOESN'T ANSWER EVERY QUESTION

I love the Bible. I've spent hundreds of hours in its pages every year for decades and it's amazing. It continues to be a source of encouragement and direction in the good times and the bad. Yet I've learned something that has become a critical thread in my understanding: the Bible doesn't answer every question.

Now I know this may sound like heresy to some, but I think we'd all agree the Bible doesn't tell us how to cook an egg or what color to paint our house. It won't tell us where we should shop or what landscaping to put in our yard. It won't tell us whether to buy a Ford or Chevy, although I think God is partial to Fords because Judges 12:5 tells us the Gileadites—sworn enemies of Israel—captured the Fords of the Jordan. They must have been hot-ticket items!

Reprograming Our Default Settings

I viewed the Bible more like a user's manual in my earlier days of following Jesus. It only made sense that if God created us, then He certainly knew how to make us work. All we had to do was follow the instructions and connect the dots. Although today I realize it's so much more, there is a great deal of truth in this. We all come into this world with a boatload of corrupted default settings and, if we don't get them reprogrammed, it will lead to a loss of peace and purpose.

By now it should be clear that redeeming is Jesus' specialty. Sin is what messed up our defaults to begin with, so getting rid of that sin is the first step. But the redemption package also includes a new power—the Holy Spirit—which is none other than God Himself! With His help we can get to work on reprogramming, and the default settings are all in the manual: the Bible. We looked briefly at Romans 12:2 in the last chapter, but let's look at it again:

> *Do not be conformed to* (pressed into the mold of) *this world, but be transformed by the renewing of your mind, so that you may prove what God's will is, that which is good and acceptable and perfect.*

This verse starts by telling us something NOT to do: don't get pressed into the mold of everything going on around you. Don't get shaped by your friends, celebrities, talk show hosts, or group chats. Don't take your values from Hollywood or social media. Don't do it! DO NOT CONFORM!

The Mind of God

That's a tall order when we're surrounded by an endless stream of impressions every day. How is it even possible? We find the answer in the middle of the verse: *BUT be transformed by the renewing of your mind.* We can keep from being conformed to the the things going on around us by reprogramming our minds with the mind of God.

Now you may say, "Hey, I don't think like everyone else. I'm not some mindless dweeb. I think for myself. I'm my own person." Probably most of us think this way, so let's try a little word association game. What comes to your mind when you think of words like success, freedom, authority, happiness, morality, marriage, money, and sex? No doubt your mind immediately went to something, and there's a good chance it wasn't original. Somebody or something has pressed you into that mold, and it's become the default for your thinking. So here's the question: Is your default the result of a conformed mind or a renewed mind?

Our defaults as followers of Jesus are not to be set by *cultural* truth, *political* truth, *my* truth, or *your* truth. They are to be set by the truth of our creator: God. And that truth is found in the Bible. Often referred to as the Word of God, it can read like a user's manual from the perspective of its objective and straightforward declarations. Should I lie? No. Should I be generous? Yes. Should I take revenge on those who hurt me? No. Should I engage in sexual relationships outside of marriage? No. Should I honor my parents? Yes. And so on. Just as sure as my car's manual tells me when and where to add oil, the instructions are clear. It is black and white objective truth.

Sometimes I hear people complain that the Bible is just so hard to understand. I get that: it can be. Yet more often the bigger problem is that it's so *easy* to understand, but we don't like what it says. Pleading ignorance won't work. We need to renew our minds with the default settings of truth from the Word of God, the Bible.

We Can't Steal What Belongs to Others

There's something important we need to understand before leaving this objective aspect of the Bible. Much of it is a narrative—especially the Old Testament—chronicling specific times, places, peoples, and events. It's fascinating as we get to see God working in real time with real people in real situations. Sometimes God gave very clear instructions to these people and, as they risked taking Him at His word, they experienced His faithfulness and reality in marvelous ways.

But we can get ourselves into a whole lot of trouble if we go around putting our names on instructions and promises given to others. There are things God told people like Abraham, Moses, Gideon, Elijah, and the

Apostles that are not for us. Anything that is repeated in the New Testament for every follower of Jesus, and anything based on the unchanging character of God is as good today as it was in the past. But we can't take something specifically given to others for the part God had for them in His story, put our name on it, and then claim it as our own.

This is what happened in the historical development of the country of South Africa. Huguenot settlers from France and Holland in the seventeenth and eighteenth centuries were convinced they were the new chosen people of God. This meant they had a divine right to the land—just as Israel had to the land of Canaan— and all the promises and instructions given to Israel belonged to them. They'd leaf through the pages of the Old Testament when faced with a decision, find something God had told the people of Israel, and take it as their own.

They savagely slaughtered thousands of indigenous peoples because God had told the Israelites to kill the Canaanites. They enslaved others and felt good about it because that's what the people of Israel had done. They allowed certain groups to live in communities within designated boundaries, but always as inferior and separate from the chosen. This ultimately led to what became known as Apartheid (apartness); institutional segregation. While it seemed unjust to many, it made perfect sense to those who felt they were the chosen of God.

We can't steal what was given to others for their part in God's story and claim it as our own.

The Ways of God

But once we move from the objective truths of the Bible, the water isn't always as clear. This is where we find ourselves wading into what is sometimes referred to as the *ways* or *principle*s of God. It's different from objective truth because it isn't spelled out as clearly and takes some processing. Just like in any relationship, the better you know someone, the better you understand how they think. If Joy asks me to pick up milk at the store without giving me the details, having known her for fifty years narrows my choices.

The longer I've been in a relationship with Jesus and been exposed to His mind through the Bible, the more I've come to understand His ways. Seeing His response to people and situations throughout the Scriptures helps me know what He honors and despises, loves and hates, what grieves Him and what brings Him joy.

When judges and priests governed the nation of Israel in its early years, one of the last in that system was Eli. He was a good man, but his sons—who served as priests under him—violated the clear instructions of God by stealing from the people and engaging in sexual immorality. Although Eli knew about it, and even corrected them, he allowed it to continue.

When God finally confronts Eli and tells him He's going to remove him from his position, He concludes with this:

Those who honor Me, I will honor, but those who despise Me will be disdained.

I Samuel 2:30

Eli had honored his sons above God, and it cost him dearly. One of the ways of God is that honoring Him in our choices has both direct and indirect benefits. While specifics and situations will vary, the principle remains unchanged. So, while you may not find an objective black and white answer to something you're looking for, there's a good chance you'll discover a principle that points you in a God-honoring direction.

One day Jesus was asked which of the Old Testament commandments was the most important, and He responded without hesitation:

Love the Lord your God with all of your heart, all your soul, all your mind, and all your strength… and love your neighbor as yourself.

Mark 12:30-31

This is the operating system of God, which means a fundamental question to ask when seeking direction is, "What does love require of me?" It's an overriding principle that applies in nearly every situation.

When Jesus was talking to a crowd about how worry and anxiety are rooted in the fear of not having enough, here's how He wrapped things up:

But seek first His kingdom and His righteousness, and all these things will be given to you as well.
                                                    Matthew 6:33

This is one of the consistent ways of God that doesn't change with time or particulars. It is as true today as it was the day it was spoken: be led by the purposes of God rather than cultural fears and pressures.

The Bible was written for all people in all times and all cultures. While the New and Old Testaments address things in historical settings with practices that no longer exist, the ways of God are the same for every generation.

So if you're looking for an answer about a particular home you're thinking of purchasing, you won't find its address spelled out in the Bible. If you're wondering which of three job offers to accept, you probably won't find the company name printed in a verse. But what you will find are the ways of God so you can ask the right questions:

- Will I be honoring God in doing this?
- Is it violating the law of love?
- Is my motive selfish?
- Am I taking the heart and purposes of God into account?

The ways of God provide a template that can be overlayed on every question we're asking. And violating these principles can knock us off course just as fast as rejecting clear black and white instructions.

Knowing God

But now we come to the best part. It was never God's intention that the Bible answer every question because, if it did, then we'd never need to talk with Him. We'd never need to pray or engage the Holy Spirit. All we'd have to do is turn to the right page and we'd be good to go. Quick, easy, and efficient.

We know as parents how discouraging it can be when it feels like our kids only interest in us is for what they can get. We're nothing more than glorified meal tickets! And while we enjoy providing them with good things, what we really want is *them.*

There were times when my kids were younger that I didn't give them things they were asking for—even though I could—simply because I wanted to spend time with them. Sometimes I'd have them work with me on a project to earn money so they could buy it themselves. I usually could have done whatever I was doing quicker by myself, but speed wasn't the objective: it was about being together.

We've got to understand that God giving quick and easy answers to our questions is certainly within His power. After all, He's God! But what He wants more than anything is US. *The purpose of the Bible is not just to help us find answers, but to help us find God.* When we understand this, the Bible comes alive in a whole new way.

This is what Jesus told a group of scholars who had been studying the Scriptures for a long time:

> *You search the Scriptures because you think that in them you have eternal life; it is these that testify about Me; and you are unwilling to come to Me so that you may have life.*

> John 5:39-40

Jesus is saying, "You've spent years searching the Scriptures for answers, but in the process, you've missed the most important thing: ME!" This means it's possible to read the Bible and completely miss God because we're only reading for information. *The purpose of the Bible is not only so we can know answers, but so we can know God.* The story He invites us into is the story of relationship.

The Heart of God

Something I've learned to ask God when I find myself in need of His direction comes from a prayer recorded in the book of Psalms:

> *Send out Your light and Your truth, let them lead me; Let them bring me to Your holy hill and to Your dwelling places.*

> Psalm 43:3

The psalmist needed help. He was committed to following God and wanted to make sure he stayed between the lines. He was asking Him to reveal His divine TRUTH, but was asking for something else: LIGHT. The *objective truth* of the Word of God might move us in the right direction, but we often find we need more than black and white. The *ways of God* might get us to the right highway, but there's still a gap. To get in the right lane we need more than truth: we need LIGHT that takes us to the very dwelling place of God.

This LIGHT doesn't come from a few hurried minutes of flipping through the Bible in search of a magic verse, because it's the Holy Spirit. It's God Himself reaching into the depths of our souls to take us where our minds alone never can. It doesn't come from approaching the Bible simply as a user's manual but as a love letter. The words sound and feel different because there's a heartbeat.

My dad, an officer in the U.S. Army, was stationed in Japan at the close of World War II as part of America's rebuilding effort. It was at a time when communication was much different than today, and the primary means of correspondence was letters—actual ink on paper sent through the mail! Anyway, he wrote my mother *every day* during the year he was away. It's hard to believe, but I still have the letters in a shoebox in my closet. I've read a number of them, and they're filled with mundane details of what was going on in his very ordinary life. Not exactly Marvel Universe thrillers.

But they were something very different to my mother because she knew the man. She was reading the words of someone she loved and who loved her. It wasn't just information, but heart. She had truth AND light because she wasn't reading a manual, but a love letter.

I think this is how God set it up for us. While the Bible is filled with all kinds of needed information, it's so much more. He wants us to feel His heartbeat in the pages, and when we do, the answers to our questions become clearer.

Hearing from God

Some say God isn't speaking anymore because the divine revelation—the Bible—has been completed. If they're saying God is no longer speaking through men and women to make authoritative statements to the world that are not found in Scripture, I agree.

But there is no question our relational God is still speaking and has been since the beginning of time. While His communication is always done against the backdrop of the Bible, you can often hear His whispers between the lines. Something is going on deep in your soul that is beyond the words. It nudges you in directions you may have never even thought about and answers questions in ways that almost surprise you. It's God. His voice travels on the waves of your mind, intellect, and emotions. He shows up in circumstances and conversations. He's not declaring revelation to the world, but He is to you. It's what happens when the Scriptures connect you not only to the words of God, but to His heart.

I got cold feet shortly after asking Joy to marry me. It wasn't that I didn't love her, because I did. It wasn't that I didn't want to marry her, because I did. It was that my recent experience with God had changed the course of my life and I didn't want anything, including marriage, to alter that. So I canceled the engagement—not just once, but seven times! I kept teetering with debilitating fear. God would confirm I should move ahead, we'd get re-engaged, then I'd break it off again. Not good.

Then early one Sunday morning I was reading in the New Testament Book of Ephesians. When I got to chapter five, I found it had a lot to say about marriage. It was like God was again saying, "Stop second-guessing what I've been telling you, move past your fears, and get married!"

A little later I picked up Joy at her house and we drove to church. The guest speaker that morning was an elderly missionary who, after apologizing for his wife's absence, spent the next ten minutes praising her value on the mission field. He couldn't have done it without her. About that time the lady sitting in front of us—who knew nothing of my struggle—turned, patted me on the knee and said, "See, it won't be so bad." That was it. God had spoken loud and clear through the Bible, the missionary, and the lady. We got married.

While the Bible is a dynamic book that communicates the words, ways, and heart of God, there is no question it has been abused for centuries to further greed and self-promotion. Some have used it to justify killing and the destruction of those they oppose. Others have taken words from the Scriptures to support strategic political actions in advancing their ambitions. And then there are those who carry around select Bible passages, ready to inflict pain and shame on any they find offensive.

There is probably something in all of us that wants to massage the words of Scripture to justify our choices. It just makes us feel better to have the Bible on our side. But if we're not careful, we may get the answer we want—but completely miss God.

Going for a Walk

There was an interesting movie released in 2007 that is one of those under-the-radar films because it's kind of quirky: *Lars and the Real Girl.* Lars, played by Ryan Gosling, is a socially awkward thirty-something who struggles with deep trauma from his childhood. One of the ways this manifests itself is in his inability to relate to girls: he's never been on a date and can't even talk with them.

So what he ends up doing is making an online purchase of an anatomically correct life-sized doll from an adult website. About now you may be thinking this is going someplace you don't want to go, but relax; it's not. That's the genius of the film.

The doll came with a detailed manual of everything he needed to know: her name (Bianca), background (Danish), parents (she's an orphan), past life (missionary on sabbatical from Brazil), allergies, food preferences, etc. Because she doesn't speak English, Lars lets everyone know what she's saying. It's strange at first, but soon everyone in town treats her like she's real. After all, she's Lar's girlfriend! She sits at meals, attends church, even gets a part-time job at the hospital and is elected to the school board.

But little by little Lars begins to sense something isn't quite right. As he looks at real girls—one in particular—he begins to feel a slight ripple of connection that he doesn't have with Bianca. At the end of the movie Bianca dies, something he lets everyone know because he's creating the reality. When the funeral is over, he turns to the girl he's been noticing and says, "You want to take a walk?" And they do.

The danger in thinking of the Bible as a magic answer book is that it can lead to an anatomically correct God. We know His name, background, likes and dislikes, but there's no real connection. We can study the manual, discuss it—even teach it—but it's lifeless.

That's because God never intended the Bible to be an end in itself. It's an incredible volume that contains objective truth we can comprehend with our minds. Although it takes more processing, the ways and principles of God can also be understood with the mind. But to really hear from God—to get answers to those questions that churn in the deepest recesses of our souls—is going to take something more. It's going to take LIGHT: a two-way connection of heart on heart that is fueled by the Spirit of God. Not a quick grab-and-go, but a slow burn.

God intentionally set it up like this because He's way more interested in a relationship than in cranking out answers. He wants us to crawl into His lap, lay our head on His chest, and listen to His heartbeat. And when we do, we find way more than an anatomically correct God. We discover a loving Father who knows our names, knows our needs, and gently says, "You want to take a walk?"

And it's then we find more than answers. We find Him.

I come to the garden alone,
While the dew is still on the roses;
And the voice I hear, falling on my ear,
The Son of God discloses.

He speaks, and the sound of His voice
Is so sweet the birds hush their singing;
And the melody that He gave to me
Within my heart is ringing.

And He walks with me, and He talks with me,
And He tells me I am His own,
And the joy we share as we tarry there,
None other has ever known.

C. Austin Miles

Chapter Eight

GOD OWES ME NOTHING, EXCEPT...

ENTITLEMENT: *the belief that one is inherently deserving of benefits, privileges, or special treatment.*

I think we just described all of us.

This kind of thinking is at the root of much of the unrest we experience at every level. We deserve better. And when we don't get what we think we're entitled to, it creates tension that affects both us and those around us. It disrupts families, businesses, governments, churches, and relationships as it divides people from one another and generates a ripple of dissatisfaction and ungratefulness.

Since the word *entitlement* can tend to sound a bit selfish and greedy, we've come up with a more politically correct term: *rights*. Everybody has rights. Life would be good if the playing field were just leveled to give equal rights and privileges to everyone. There are whole philosophies of government built on this ideal: no one is above another, and everyone is entitled to the same benefits and opportunities. It's a utopia—at least on paper.

Yet history tells us this never works. Even when there is so-called equality, there are always those who are just a little more equal than others. That's because nobody really wants to be equal; they want to be a step above. It's human nature. It seems the only ones pushing for "equality" are those who find themselves below the waterline. But once they move up, it's not long before they use their new place in the pecking order to suppress those under them. It's the history of the world and has been going on for a very long time. True social equality is impossible because human nature won't allow it.

Israel's King Solomon had insight into this dilemma nearly three thousand years ago that was way ahead of his time:

> Under three things the earth quakes, and under four, it cannot endure: Under a slave when he becomes king, and a fool when he is satisfied with food; Under an unloved woman when she gets a husband, and a female servant when she dispossesses her mistress.
>
> Proverbs 30:21-24

Solomon is saying that when those who are lower find a way to move up, it's not long before they use their new position to lord it over those who were once above them. There is a sinister enjoyment in having the advantage and turning the tables.

There's no question that serious inequities exist in both opportunities and freedoms that must be addressed socially and politically. Wrongs that have been culturally accepted need to be righted and changes made. But let's not kid ourselves to think this will solve the world's problems because, no matter how you cut it, everyone thinks they're entitled to more. We're a tough crowd to please.

My mother used to quote a little poem to my brother and me when we were young:

As a rule a man's a fool,
When it's hot he wants it cool,
When it's cool he wants it hot,
Always wanting what is not,
Wanting more than what he's got.

I can't figure out why she would say this to two happy, non-complaining children like my brother and me!?

Entitlement Issues with God

But entitlement isn't only about culture and politics. Most people have entitlement issues with God: He owes them more. No matter what He's done in the past, it's never enough. The glass is always half-empty and, if God doesn't fill it the way they think He should, they might not like Him anymore. Maybe they'll even stop believing in Him!

Those who were to become the nation of Israel were not happy as they found themselves living as slaves in Egypt. They were poorly treated, worked to the bone, had no hope for the future, and were without a country. It just wasn't fair. If they were truly God's people, He owed them more. Then things began to look up as they left Egypt under Moses' leadership for a land that was to be their own. They liked Moses, they liked God, and they were grateful. Life was good!

But as the wear and tear of the journey took its toll, they began to complain; Was this the best God could do? They deserved better. They complained about Moses, saying they should be equal with him in decision-making. They complained about the living conditions; water shortages and the dangers of the desert. And they complained about the diet. They'd had a delicious array of food choices in Egypt, but now it was nothing but this manna stuff day in and day out. How many ways can you fix manna? They were no longer slaves and were about to rule their own country, but the current conditions were unacceptable. They didn't like Moses and didn't like God. So there!

It's hard to be too critical of these nomadic wanderers because most of us think the same way. Time has a way of eroding our memories and present realities move us to demand more. So let's talk about the elephant in the room.

What Does God Owe Us?

As we've seen in earlier chapters, in the beginning God made everything just how he wanted it and then placed His crown jewel—people—into HIS world. But things deteriorated when they didn't trust Him and wanted to control the sandbox. Because He had given them the freedom to make their own choices, He allowed them to do it, but it cost Him greatly. His redemptive plan took Him from heaven to the cross, where He paid for all our wrongdoing. He then offered forgiveness and a forever loving relationship with Him as a gift. God owed us punishment, but gave us grace.

When I owned a company in Florida that had a division in Texas, I had employees in Houston who managed that part of the business. It involved the collecting of cash throughout the city on a regular basis, and the policy was that no money was ever to be kept in vehicles or personal homes overnight. It was to be in the bank before the close of business.

One day I got a call from an employee who told me $5,000 of company money had been stolen from his home. He'd picked it up late in the day and hadn't been able to make it to the bank in time. He was very remorseful and apologetic. But as he continued to talk, something began to sound a little off, so I decided to fly to Houston and check things out.

The next day I took him and his wife to a nice restaurant to thank them for the good job he'd been doing. Then, when the employee got up to use the restroom, his wife just couldn't take it anymore. Through her tears she told me of how they'd run into hard times and had taken the money. She let him know when he returned that the cat was out of the bag, and he knew it was the end of the line.

I did some quick processing as we sat there, and then did the strangest thing: I decided not to fire him. I knew they needed the income and life would be a whole lot harder if he were unemployed. Over time He would have to pay back what he'd taken, but he'd still have a job. He was extended grace and was unbelievably grateful. I didn't owe him that. He'd crossed the line and deserved to be out.

Once people chose to turn their back on God and go their own way, God owed them nothing. They'd stolen from Him, disrespected Him, and didn't trust Him. And it wasn't just humanity in general that did this: it was me.

I worked and studied hard as a student—especially in high school and college—because grades were very important to me. High achievement was part of my identity and doing poorly was devastating and unacceptable. So when I'd get a grade lower than I thought I deserved, guess who I'd blame? Yeah, God. I'd done my part by studying, but He hadn't done His—even though I'd asked Him to. So I'd curse Him and tell Him to go to hell. I didn't need Him if that was the best He could do.

I deserved His wrath, but that isn't what I got. He extended grace. A few years later I received His gift of forgiveness and stepped into a loving relationship with the infinite-personal God. I have been grateful ever since.

I am constantly amazed at those who get so angry at the God they've rejected. Even though they want nothing to do with Him, they still feel He's indebted to them because…because…well, just because. It's entitlement.

Slammed

I was hit with something in the summer of 2020 that took me to one of the most challenging places of my life. On the morning of July 7, I felt like I had something in my eye—kind of like sawdust—which made sense because I was working on a construction project at the house. But it didn't go away and continued to worsen throughout the day. The next morning found me at our family doctor, and then on to the ophthalmologist (eye specialist). The diagnosis?   Shingles on the cornea of my eye.

Soon it spread over the left side of my face and head, and within two weeks the lights went out— literally. Exposure to any light, and even the slightest movement of my eye triggered intense head pain that was unlike anything I'd ever experienced.

I lay motionless in the darkness of my room for the next five weeks: no lamps or screens or light of any kind (TV, computer, phone). The slightest movement brought brain freeze pain that made my head feel like it would explode at any moment. At one point Joy feared I was having a brain aneurysm and rushed me to the hospital. For several weeks she ground my food because the pressure of chewing sky-rocketed the pain. Day after day there was not the slightest change.

Then in the sixth week there was a small improvement, and over the next few days I began to move around a bit. By mid-September I was able to do a little work on my construction project, but it was slow: twenty minutes of work and twenty minutes of rest. I was very weak and still sensitive to light.

Delayed Insights

Once I was able to function with a degree of normalcy, several asked if God had taught me anything in the darkness. The answer was no. It was all I could do to just get through the next five minutes...then the next five...and the next five. Nothing heroic or spiritual. But those minutes slowly added up to hours, then days, then weeks, and today I'm writing about it.

I was reading the Sermon on the Mount in the Gospel of Matthew one morning after I'd made it back to the land of the living. Jesus wraps up His discourse with a story of two houses: one built on a foundation of sand, the other of rock. It's recorded in Matthew 7. The narrative tells us that both houses took a severe hit from a storm:

The rain fell and the floods came, and the winds blew and slammed against that house; and yet it did not fall, for it had been founded on the rock… everyone who hears these words of Mine, and does not act on them, will be like a foolish man who built his house on the sand…the rain fell and the floods came, and the winds blew and slammed against that house; and it fell—and its collapse was great.

Matthew 7:25-27

The same violent forces slammed both houses, but only the one built on a foundation of rock stood. And then something began to dawn on me. I had been violently slammed but was still standing! I was not cursing God or angry at those around me. I wasn't throwing a pity party, shaking my fist, or saying life wasn't fair. I'd lost nearly two months of my life, yet even in the darkness I had lived with a restful soul. I had built on the right foundation. Thank You, Jesus!

A little later I was reading one of Peter's letters in the New Testament and these words jumped off the page:

…knowing that you were not redeemed with perishable things like silver or gold from your futile way of life inherited from your forefathers, but with precious blood, as of a lamb unblemished and spotless, the blood of Christ.

1 Peter 1:18-19

I began to see that if I *really* understood what Jesus had done to redeem me—that He hadn't purchased my redemption with something cheap like silver or gold, but with His very life—I would never again feel I was entitled to another thing. People had been praying for me, yet from where I lay I wasn't sure it had changed anything. Had God let me down? Did He owe me answered prayer? Did He owe me healing? Is that what my faith was based on? Should I be mad at Him because He didn't do more and let me suffer? Should I stop believing in Him?

And then it hit me. If I said I was entitled to answered prayer—or anything else for that matter—then I'd be saying the cross wasn't enough. His resurrection wasn't enough. My imperishable inheritance of eternity in heaven wasn't enough. I still deserved more.

Even as I write these words, I feel an overwhelming sense of shame that after all He's done, I would ever think for a single moment that it wasn't enough. He's already gone the distance and paid the ultimate price. I've been redeemed by His grace, am a child of the living God, and live every day immersed in the love of my heavenly Father. Anything more is gravy, and while I love gravy, if I never get another drop, He's already done more than enough.

Now to the King eternal, immortal, invisible, the only God, be honor and glory forever and ever. Amen.

I Timothy 1:17

Are you good on this? I hope so, because if you're not there's little reason to go any further. You'll live with a chip on your shoulder and end up missing the incredible life God has for you in His story between now and the grave.

What About Prayer?

Then where does prayer fit in? Isn't it our way of communicating with God so we can get what we want? Doesn't He at least owe us that? Not exactly. As powerful as prayer is, it can sometimes be both confusing and unnecessary. Track with me on this for a minute.

We seem to get conflicting messages when we read about prayer in the Bible. In one place we're told that if we ask for anything in His name we'll get it, but later we're told we only get what we ask if it's according to His will. Then we're told we don't get what we ask because we ask with wrong motives, but we also don't get what we want because we don't ask at all. Later we're told that prayer is powerful and accomplishes much, yet when Jesus asked His Father about foregoing the cross, His request was denied. A lot is going on here. So, does God owe us answers to our prayers?

Many excellent books have been written on this, and I know the previous statements all blend perfectly in God's divine timing and understanding. The point here, however, is not to engage in a theological discussion of prayer but to help us better understand what we can expect from God.

For starters, sometimes prayer is downright un-necessary. If God has already promised us something or already made something clear, we don't need to pray about it. As a follower of Jesus, I never ask Him to be with me because He's already told me He is. I never ask Him to love me because He's already assured me He does. I never invite God into my presence because He was here long before I was. I never ask God to forgive me because He's already guaranteed me He has. I frequently thank Him for each of these, but never ask Him to do what He's already promised.

I know this might create uneasiness for some, but don't lose the point. I fully expect God to do what He's said He will, so instead of asking, I thank Him for being true to His word. This turns me into a trusting, grateful, faith-filled person who lives in the joy and wonder of His love.

Then there are times when our prayers don't matter because God in His sovereignty has already determined what He's going to do. The cross was a foregone conclusion, as is the death of every person and the coming and going of seasons. God has already determined His will and our prayers won't change it.

But then there are those situations where our prayers make a huge difference. After reading the words of James 4:2 many years ago, "You don't have because You don't ask," I made the decision to ask all the time for things He hasn't already promised. I don't worry about trying to sort out if it's God's will or if my motives are right. I just ask because I never want to get to heaven, question God as to why He didn't do this or that, only to have Him say, "I would have loved to, Ron, but you just never asked!" So, I ask.

I asked God for a boy when Joy and I were thinking about having children and sure enough, we had a boy. When we wanted another child, I again asked God for a boy and got a boy. But when Joy was pregnant for the third time, I realized I hadn't asked God for what I wanted, which was a girl. So I asked, and we had a girl. Now I'm sure you're thinking, "Come on, she was already pregnant. Do you honestly think God will change the gender of a child several months into pregnancy?" I don't know; it didn't matter. I just knew I never wanted God to say I didn't have because I didn't ask. So, did God answer my prayer? I think yes, but only He knows.

Here's what we can expect from God when it comes to prayer. First of all, we can expect Him to listen. Even if He already knows what He's going to do, He still loves to hear our voices. He loves that we trust Him enough to include Him in our decisions. Engaging with God in prayer is a huge relationship builder.

Secondly, there's usually no way we can know if our prayers fall into the category of things God has already set in stone or something He's ready and willing to act on if we only ask. That's why it's good to make our requests with great boldness and leave the outcome to Him. We're not entitled to get whatever we ask, and thinking we are puts us on a path to disappointment and bitterness. We are entitled to ask Him whatever we want because that's what children do, but the outcome is up to Him. His answers, both yes and no, are always connected to the part He is writing for us in His story. In God we trust.

In Jesus We Get Everything

What we get when we come into a relationship with Jesus is not a bag full of goodies, but HIM! He is the whole package and, through the Holy Spirit, He is with us every minute of every day. He owes us nothing because in Him, we already possess everything.

For in Him all the fullness of Deity dwells in bodily form, and in Him, you have been made complete…

Colossians 2:9-10

What then shall we say to these things? If God is for us, who is against us? He who did not spare His own Son, but delivered Him over for us all, how will He not also with Him freely give us all things?

Romans 8:31-32

I know how to get along with little, and I also know how to live in prosperity; in any and every circumstance I have learned the secret of being filled and going hungry, both of having abundance and suffering need. I can do all things through Him who strengthens me.

Philippians 4:12-13

God has given us all He is, which is the sum total of all we need. But when we begin to doubt His love and think He's holding out on us, we end up making foolish choices that take us where we don't want to go.

Coming Full Circle

I had given my Texas employee what he didn't deserve: grace. I had made it possible for him to keep his job and enjoy a steady stream of income. As long as he was connected to me, he was good.

A year later, money again ended up missing: $8,000. This time he said it had been taken from his truck while he was having lunch. This time I involved the police, who uncovered that it was an inside arrangement he had worked with a friend. And this time it cost him his job and all his benefits.

Even after all he'd been given, he still thought he deserved more. The earlier gratitude had faded, and now he felt justified in taking what wasn't his. But in the end, it cost him way more than he bargained for.

One of the threads I've worked hard to weave into the fabric of my life is that God owes me nothing. This is why I've made it a habit for many years to start every day by thanking Him for the many ways He's blessed me. I am a beloved child of the living God and want to live with a healthy soul of gratitude rather than entitlement. He owes me nothing because in Him, I already have everything.

Thank You, Jesus!

Amazing grace how sweet the sound
That saved a wretch like me!
I once was lost, but now am found,
Was blind, but now I see.

Through many dangers, toils and snares
I have already come:
'Tis grace has brought me safe thus far,
And grace will lead me home.

The Lord has promised good to me,
His word my hope secures;
He will my shield and portion be
As long as life endures.

John Newton

Chapter Nine

THE BEST IS YET TO COME

I was diagnosed with cancer in early 2009. Though the prognosis was for a complete recovery, I knew even the mention of the C-word could create anxiety in those close to me. So I put off telling anyone for a week, then another…and another. Finally, I knew I had to at least tell my family. I figured my four boys would be fine because, after all, they were men. But the one I was most worried about was my daughter. She and I were close with a kind of specialness that only exists between dads and daughters.

I broke the news as optimistically as I could: no big deal, a slight bump in the road, things are going to be fine. I got the reaction I expected from the boys, but it was my daughter who surprised me. "Dad," she said, "If you die, I'm really going to miss you. But knowing how much you're looking forward to heaven, I'll be happy for you." She got it! The best is what comes on the other side of the grave.

This has been a thread of my life for many years and has changed the way I look at today, tomorrow, and forever. It is woven throughout the pages of the Bible and is at the core of much of Jesus' teaching.

When the Apostle Paul talks about the wisdom of God, He calls it a *mystery* that can't be understood with the limitations of human reasoning (1 Corinthians 2:6-7). Part of this mystery is what God has in store for those who are followers of Jesus:

> *No eye has seen, no ear has heard, and no mind has imagined what God has prepared for those who love Him.*

> I Corinthians 2:9 NLT

Much of the New Testament is spent detailing the earth piece of this *mystery,* yet we're given only glimpses of the heaven piece. I think that's because it defies human explanation, is out of this world, and is better than anything we can imagine. It's the best of the best on steroids. It's what people say when they've experienced something so good they can't find words to describe it: "I thought I'd died and gone to heaven."

As much as we enjoy this life, it doesn't take rocket science to know that something isn't right. Children are starving in a world of abundance. The innocent are abused as the guilty walk free. Families are divided, children are abandoned, and disease sucks the life from good people. We long for a place where everything is good and right. Heaven is that place.

The first thing most people think about when it comes to heaven is the living conditions. In Florida we have what we call snowbirds: those who live in the north during Florida's hot and humid months, then migrate south when the arctic winds blow cold and snowy. It's the best of both worlds. Although the Bible doesn't specifically talk about this, I can't imagine it's too far off: the best of Florida and Michigan without politics.

Everything New

What the Bible does tell us about heaven is something we looked at in Chapter Four:

> *He* (Jesus) *will wipe every tear from their eyes. There will be no more death or mourning or crying or pain, for the old order of things has passed away. He who was seated on the throne said, "I am making everything new!"*

> Revelation 21:4-5 NIV

Think for a moment of what it is that brings tears to your eyes: physical injury, disappointment, betrayal, loss of possessions, loss of relationships, broken dreams, hopelessness, fear, and the death of those we love. Can you think of more? I'm sure you can. The older I get, the more I realize that some of the things that cut into my soul are never going away as long as

I'm a resident of planet earth. Many of you reading these pages live with deep hurts that reside just below the surface of your smiling face. You work hard to keep a positive attitude—getting needed help from counseling and support groups—but it's always there. Some of you are dealing with physical and emotional pain every day, knowing the best you can hope for is that it be controlled as you learn to live with it.

But the best is yet to come because Jesus is going to make everything new. Heaven will be pain-free, medication-free, arthritis-free, feeding-tube-free, and wheel-chair-free. There will be no more counting of calories or fat grams or carbs. There will be no more Special Olympics or special needs children, no more anxious waiting rooms, ultra-sounds, or caskets. No more divorce papers, betrayals, or heartbreaks. The very hand that shaped the wonders of this earth will wipe away every tear, forever.

As I write these words, I live in a body that is moving south, and I don't mean for the winter. I'm past the age where things are getting better. One hip has already been replaced and the other surgically repaired. I have less strength and endurance than I did thirty years ago. My mind is still sharp—or so I think—but there's a good chance that in time, that too will deteriorate. This is how it was set up to work from the very beginning for all earth-dwellers. But the best is yet to come.

We'll enjoy friendships in heaven that are not tarnished by imperfection. Have you ever noticed how most advertising is done in the context of relationships? Cars, food, beer, electronics, building supplies, medications, and just about anything you can think of is framed by the enjoyment of doing life with others.

We all crave relationships, which is a reflection of being created in the image of a relational God. Yet our imperfections and the imperfections of others lead to painful breakdowns that put a hole in our souls. This will never happen in heaven because there will be no sin. The best is yet to come.

But the main attraction of heaven will be Jesus. He alone will have center stage because everything we've ever enjoyed—or ever will enjoy—comes from who He is and what He's done. His closest followers had come to realize this and were filled with sadness when He told them He was going to be leaving. Then He added something that gave them hope:

> *I am going to prepare a place for you. And if I go and prepare a place for you, I am coming again and will take you to Myself, so that where I am, there you also will be.*
>
> John 14:2-3

Heaven is where we'll be together with Jesus and one another forever. Faith will no longer be necessary because we'll see Him face to face. There will be no more doubt, praying, Bible studies, or wondering if we got it right. Heaven is where Jesus is, and those who don't want anything to do with Him will get their wish: they won't be there.

Finish Line Thinking

I've never been much of a runner, but I dabbled in it a little when I was working with students at Texas A&M. I set a goal to run the Straight Shot (6.2 miles) because I figured it would help if I had an objective. I trained for several months, and when the day of the race came, I was psyched. Friends and family were positioned along the route to cheer me on. Even though I didn't finish in the top ten—or even the top one hundred— for me it was a win because I went the distance and finished in the time I had set.

Yet without question, my goal from the very beginning was to cross the finish line. There was no way I wanted to keep running forever. I entered the race to go the distance and be done, and when I did, I was so done that I've never run another one!

I usually watch at least part of the marathon (26.2 miles) in the Summer Olympics because I'm in awe of such human endurance. Mile after mile the runners pace themselves, and when they finally cross the finish line, they've got nothing left in the tank. I don't remember ever hearing any of them say, "I only wish the race had been longer...I wish I could have just kept going and going." They entered the race knowing there was an end. And at the end—not in the middle—came the celebration.

All of us are born into this world with an expiration date stamped on our bodies that is visible only to God. King David tells us that everyone who enters this life is given a predetermined number of days (Psalm 139:16). While some may have more than others, nobody has an unlimited supply. The day we are born is the day the countdown begins, and every day moves us one step closer to the finish line.

There's something about finish lines that change the way we think and live. A few years back, Tim McGraw's "Live Like You Were Dying" spent seven weeks at #1 on Billboard's Hot Country Songs. The basic message was simple: figure out what's important and begin living it now.

But Moses had a hit single many years earlier, recorded in Psalm 90, that carried the same message in the form of a prayer:

Teach us to number our days, that we may gain a heart of wisdom.

Psalm 90:12 NIV

If we don't think in terms of finish lines it's easy to make foolish choices. We forget the best is yet to come and begin living like it's only about the here and now. Schlitz Beer captured this in a series of television commercials that showed friends enjoying one another around ice-cold Schlitz, then adding, "You only go around once in life, so you've got to grab for all the gusto you can." It's all about today.

A classic experiment was done in the early seventies known as the Marshmallow Test. It began by taking a group of preschoolers and placing a marshmallow in front of each child. The one leading the exercise then said he had to run an errand, but if they waited until he got back to eat their mallow, they'd get two. There ended up being two groups: *eat the marshmallow now* and *wait and get more later*.

They tracked these kids for a number of years, and the outcome was remarkable. The *wait and get more later* group was superior in almost every area—academics, careers, relationships—than the *eat the marshmallow now* group. If they had been able to track the results into eternity, they'd have found the same.

The thread that runs throughout the Bible is that choices made with eternity in mind always have the best outcome. This was true of Jesus:

> ...*let's run with endurance the race that is set before us, looking only at Jesus, the originator and perfecter of the faith, who for the joy set before Him endured the cross, despising the shame, and has sat down at the right hand of the throne of God.*
> Hebrews 12:1-2

We saw in Chapter Two that Satan's objective in tempting Jesus was to get Him to join the grab the marshmallow now group with no thought of the future. But it was knowing the best was yet to come that kept Him pressing through the challenges of the cross.

Making Adjustments

Thinking like this can be a real struggle when we're surrounded by present realities ever day.

Most NFL teams watch film of their previous game early in the week. Their goal is to make it to the Super Bowl, and watching the film—as painful as it may be—helps them make adjustments while there's still time. It's all about making changes in the present with the future in mind.

One of my favorite passages of Scripture for keeping this focus is I Corinthians 3:12-15. After talking about the foundation of our lives, which is Jesus, the Apostle Paul uses verbal imagery to draw attention to how today's choices affect the future:

Now, if anyone builds on the foundation (Jesus) *with gold, silver, precious stones, wood, hay, or straw, each one's work will become evident; for the day will show it because it is to be revealed with fire, and the fire itself will test the quality of each one's work. If anyone's work which he has built on it remains, he will receive a reward. If anyone's work is burned up, he will suffer loss; but he himself will be saved…*

This is like futuristic game tape of our lives so we can make adjustments while there's still time. It talks about things that last and things that don't. It talks about rewards and losses. And regardless of our understanding of these, we can all agree that rewards are good and losses are bad.

This tells us there are things we can do with our lives—wood, hay, straw—that have no value beyond the grave and will be gone forever. Then there are other things—gold, silver, precious stones—that have great value because their reward transcends this life into eternity.

Jesus gave us a clue to the kinds of things that fall into the *eternal value* category when He talked about investing in things that matter:

> *Do not store up for yourselves treasures on earth, where moth and rust destroy, and where thieves break in and steal. But store up for yourselves treasures in heaven, where neither moth nor rust destroys, and where thieves do not break in or steal; for where your treasure is, there your heart will also be.*

Matthew 6:19-21

Future value is directly connected to things that can't be destroyed by the elements or taken by thieves. Nothing in my house falls into that category. The only things with that kind of value are living souls created in God's image. That's where Jesus put His focus, and the closer we walk with Him, the more we want to do the same. Every investment made in the life of another person is matched by a deposit in the Bank of Heaven, where the rate of return only goes up.

We started this chapter by reminding ourselves that in the new order of heaven, Jesus will wipe away every tear. But I can't help but wonder if some of the tears will be from watching the game film of our lives and realizing we played to the wrong audience. There will be a sense of loss and regret. But then those tears, too, will be wiped away as we enter into the eternal joys of heaven. God wants us to look at the game tape of our lives NOW so we can make adjustments that will affect both today and forever.

Benefiting Our World

It's been argued by some that living from the perspective of *the best is yet to come* is a demotivation for doing good in the present. This is why Karl Marx, the German sociologist and economic theorist, called religion the opium of the people. His objection was that focusing on the eternal causes people to tolerate oppression and exploitation in the present, which hinders progress. It's the modern-day adage that "People can be so heavenly-minded they're of no earthly good."

Yet this is far from what the Bible teaches. In fact, it's just the opposite. If people are truly heavenly-minded, they do a whole lot of earthly good!

The Apostle Paul was having an argument with himself while locked in a Roman prison for his advancing of the good news of Jesus: Would it be better to live or die? Sounds a bit strange, but here's his reasoning:

I am torn between the two: I desire to depart and be with Christ, which is better by far; but it is more necessary for you that I remain in the body. Convinced of this, I know that I will remain…

Philippians 1:23-25 NIV

He's saying it's a no-brainer that heaven would be far better. End of discussion. But if it would be more beneficial to *others* for him to stay around a little longer, he'd be willing to put the best on hold.

When the people of Israel were exiled from their land by the Babylonians hundreds of years before Jesus, most thought it would be only a short time before they returned. So their game plan was to just chill and wait it out. Then the prophet Jeremiah gave them a wake-up call: it was going to be seventy years before they made it back, so they needed to take things up a notch and build houses, plant gardens, and raise families. Then he adds:

Seek the peace and prosperity of the city to which I have carried you into exile. Pray to the Lord for it, because if it prospers, you too will prosper.

Jeremiah 29:7 NIV

He's telling them, "Hey, don't just sit around thinking about how much better it's going to be when you finally get back to Israel. That's selfish. You're the people of God so act like it! Benefit those around you and, in the process, you too will be blessed."

Living from a perspective of future value moves us toward benefiting those around us, not away. Yet living like this can be inconvenient because it takes time, money, and effort. That's why we need to keep our souls refreshed in the truth and love of God: the best is yet to come.

Living with the future in mind doesn't mean we're unaffected by the present. We are, and sometimes it really hurts. We are active participants in the joys and limitations of being earth-dwellers. We grieve deeply in death and weep in loss. We cheer our victories and lament our defeats. We love beginnings and struggle with endings. We work, create, laugh, build, and often live with perplexity and confusion. But we also live with a hope that flows through every fiber of our being: no matter what happens today, it's not the end. The best is yet to come.

The Inheritance Package

Most of the New Testament letters were written to those working to integrate the realities of their faith into everyday life. Some found themselves being mistreated and even shunned for being followers of Jesus. That's why nearly every letter reminds them of the certainty of heaven: Don't cave under the pressure because the best is yet to come. Let's look at two of these as we conclude the chapter.

The first is from the Apostle Paul, who often let his readers know that his life had its challenges.

Five times I received from the Jews the forty lashes minus one. Three times I was beaten with rods, once I was pelted with stones, three times I was shipwrecked, I spent a night and a day in the open sea, I have been constantly on the move. I have been in danger from rivers, in danger from bandits, in danger from my fellow Jews, in danger from Gentiles; in danger in the city, in danger in the country, in danger at sea; and in danger from false believers. I have labored and toiled and have often gone without sleep; I have known hunger and thirst and have often gone without food; I have been cold and naked.

2 Corinthians 11:24-27 NIV

Sounds like he needed a different job! Yet this was the life he'd embraced as a follower of Jesus in the part God had for him in His story. Once he understood and had experienced the depths of what Jesus had done for him, he signed on as a lifer. So just what was it that kept him going in all the adversity? He tells us earlier in the letter:

Therefore, we do not lose heart. Though outwardly we are wasting away, yet inwardly we are being renewed day by day. For our light and momentary troubles are achieving for us an eternal glory that far outweighs them all. So we fix our eyes, not on what is seen, but on what is unseen, since what is seen is temporary, but what is unseen is eternal.

2 Corinthians 4:16-18 NIV

Don't you just love what he calls light troubles? The reality of his humanity was that it was in a state of decline, and every day brought him one step closer to the finish line. But he was still in the race, and knowing the best was yet to come is what kept him going. He reminded himself that everything he was experiencing, as painful as it was, was only temporary. The payoff was going to be huge, and that's where he fixed his eyes.

The second is found in the first of Peter's two letters where he addresses Christians who had been suffering for their faith. Before he gets into the meat of what he wants to talk to them about, he sets the stage:

> *Blessed be the God and Father of our Lord Jesus Christ, who according to His great mercy has caused us to be born again to a living hope through the resurrection of Jesus Christ from the dead, to obtain an inheritance which is imperishable, undefiled, and will not fade away, reserved in heaven for you, who are protected by the power of God through faith for a salvation ready to be revealed in the last time.*
>
> I Peter 1:3-5

Peter is reminding his readers that their salvation is so much greater than the here and now. It includes an inheritance package with their name on it. It's imperishable, exponentially better than anything they have ever experienced, and is backed by the power of God Himself. If they fail to remember this, some of the things he is about to tell them won't make sense.

Being a follower of Jesus can get confusing if we forget about the inheritance piece. Some of what Jesus and the Biblical writers say just won't make sense because they're written from the perspective that God has saved the best for last. Knowing this affects how we live as earth-dwellers.

- Every day brings us one step closer to the finish line.

- Every day brings us one step closer to the win.

And every day brings us one step closer to the celebration that will go on forever…and ever…and ever…

To the old rugged cross I will ever be true,
It's shame and reproach gladly bear;
Then He'll call me some day,
To my home far away,
Where His glory forever I'll share.

So I'll cherish the old rugged cross,
Till my trophies at last I lay down;
I will cling to the old rugged cross,
And exchange it some day for a crown.

George Bennard

Chapter Ten

CHOOSING FAITH OVER DOUBT

I love to build things. My trusty tool belt hung on a nail in the garage for nearly three decades, ready to join me at a moment's notice. But about a year ago it began to show its age: some of the stitching was breaking, and the leather had torn in several critical places. Yet I just couldn't part with it, so I asked Joy if she could work her magic with needle and thread to extend its life. When the next project came along, I strapped it on and off we went. But little by little it began to unravel, and the day finally came when we had to part. The threads just weren't strong enough.

Each of us is held together by a network of invisible threads that form the inner fabric of our lives, and the quality of these threads determines our story. While there are many to choose from, not all are created equal. Every thread in thread-world is assigned a tensile strength rating that gauges the stress it can withstand before breaking. Natural silk thread has the highest rating, and wool the lowest.

I've had a front-row seat as a pastor to see the tensile strength of many people. I've seen some who appeared so strong for so long, then a broken heart or a broken relationship or a broken body brought it all crashing down. That's not to minimize the stress these kinds of traumas put on any thread, but some break while others don't. I've also seen those who have been stretched far beyond anything I've ever experienced, yet held strong. All threads are not created equal.

Nearly fifty years ago I began to weave some threads into the fabric of my life. At the time I didn't know if they would be strong enough to withstand the realities of real-world pressures: raising a family, economic uncertainties, loss of possessions and friends, financial challenges, deterioration of health, death, misunderstandings, bad choices, and all the things that go with being an earth-dweller. Some around me said my God threads wouldn't hold, while others said they would. But the decision was mine to make, and I did. I became a follower of Jesus—and they've held.

I've come to understand that the *God threads* are not simply a collection of independent strands but a tapestry where each thread is tightly interwoven with the others. Christianity is not simply a *belief* in Jesus—a term often misused and misunderstood—but a weaving of the threads of the reality and love of God in and around every area of our lives. Only then can we live with a healthy soul of peace and purpose that is alive and moving in the story God has for us.

God Is Not Santa Claus

One of my objectives in writing this book was to provide a clearer understanding of how the unchanging reality of God intersects with the chaotic realities of everyday life. I've often thought that if people could only know the God I know, they'd fall in love with Him in a heartbeat. But many have had their understandings twisted and distorted—even by the church—leading to disappointment, anger, and for some a shattering of their faith.

Lots of people like the "forgiveness of sins" Jesus, the "go to heaven when I die" Jesus, and the "now I'll get everything on my Christmas list" Jesus. They like the Jesus who will give them a better marriage, better job, better finances, better family, and an easier life. Who wouldn't? But this is an imaginary Santa Claus Jesus that is all about WHAT I get. And when the WHATS fail to turn out the way they think they should, they get disillusioned and don't like Santa Claus anymore.

God is not Santa Claus. He's not someone we can create and then unbelieve out of existence if He doesn't do our bidding. *Our beliefs don't make or destroy God.* He is the creator of the ground we walk on, the water we drink, the air we breathe, and can dump us out of His sandbox any time He wants. God is not a WHAT but a WHO, and the miracle of miracles is that He wants us as His friends. I became His friend many years ago, and it's been the journey of a lifetime.

Weaving a Fabric of Rest

We talked in the first chapter about living with a *rest of soul* that comes from experiencing the very real presence and love of God. The fabric that makes this kind of life possible is one that is woven with some critical threads:

- I'm responsible for me and need to arrange the pieces of my life to keep my soul healthy.

- I play to the audience of God alone because, in the end, His applause is the only one that matters.

- God is always up to something and I can trust Him, even when I lack sufficient information to understand what it is.

- This is not heaven, and while the realities of earth dwelling may be perplexing and painful, I'll never face them without the very real presence of God.

- God loves the world so much that He gave it ME to be a conduit of His grace and love to others.

- God loves the world so much that He gave it the church—which includes me—to be the delivery system of the fullness of Jesus: Redemption, Restoration, Distribution.

- The purpose of the Bible is not only so I can know answers, but so I can know God.

- God owes me nothing because in Jesus, I already have everything.
- The best is yet to come, and knowing the celebration begins at the finish line affects how I run the race today.

Weaving these critical threads into the fabric of our souls introduces us to a life of peace and purpose. It's not simply a *belief* in Jesus, but a daily living in the joy of His friendship and love.

Living with Doubt

But is it possible that the *effects* and *invisible realities* of God I've spoken about in these pages could be attributed to coincidence or luck? I guess that's a possibility. Yet coincidence and luck are nothing more than alternate forms of faith. Webster defines *luck* as "a force that brings good fortune or adversity," and *coincidence* as "the occurrence of events that happen at the same time by accident, but seem to have some connection."

There is absolutely no way to prove the existence of either a "force" of luck or an "accident" of simultaneous connecting events. These are simply alternative faith paths to try and explain the unexplainable without God. But why? Does believing in meaningless chance give more hope and peace than the involvement of a personal God who created us, loves us, knows our names, and is for us? Does it give us a greater sense of value and purpose and destiny?

Over the years I've been asked by some, "But what if you're wrong? What if the invisible God-threads you claim are at the core of your life are simply things you've made up to make you feel better?" That's a fair question because, while I'm a person of faith, I find I am also a person of doubt. Sometimes life's realities are just so ugly and overwhelming that it makes me want to join the doubter crowd and shout, "Where is God? If He's real and loving, why doesn't He do something!"

I've never seen God with my eyes or heard Him with my ears, which is fertile soil for doubt. So is doubt a disqualifier of faith? I don't think so. Doubt is about *questioning*, while unbelief is about *rejection*. It's pretty normal to question things we don't understand, and there is a long list of things I don't understand about God. Yet this is to be expected because there is no way my little two-cylinder brain can possibly comprehend all there is to know about the infinite God:

> *"My thoughts are not your thoughts, nor are your ways My ways," declares the LORD. "For as the heavens are higher than the earth, so are My ways higher than your ways and My thoughts than your thoughts."*
>
> Isaiah 55:8

I often find myself doubting—questioning—both before and after making a decision. Just the other day I had to buy a computer monitor because mine was done. I searched the web for endorsements, only to find a plethora of differing opinions. I prayed that God would help me find the right one, but in the end I had to make a choice.

Did I get the best one for the money? Maybe yes, maybe no. Did God lead me in my search? I think yes, but I can't prove it. Yet today my new monitor is connected and working fine. My doubt didn't disqualify me from making a choice but instead drove me to investigate, process, question, and then move forward *with my doubts* to a conclusion.

I know some may question the existence of God because He hasn't performed the way they were led to believe He would. In all my years of engaging with atheists, I don't think I've ever spoken with one who started out that way. There was a time when they felt there had to be *something* out there bigger than themselves, but the unfiltered chaos of life extinguished the spark. Disappointment, loss, the hypocrisy of so-called Christians, and the seeming absence of divine intervention in times of need brought them to the conclusion God didn't exist.

Like so many others, I've experienced frustration, disappointment, and even anger at the silence of God. Life's not going the way I think it should and the darkness just keeps getting darker. It is very disorienting. And it's in times like these that I have to make a choice: will I go with faith or with doubt?

One of the things I've come to understand is that both faith and doubt are necessary for life to work. That's because for every right answer, there are a lot more wrong ones. If we never doubt, we'll end up falling for anything. But if we never have faith, we'll live in a perpetual state of despair and get frozen in time. There are very few decisions any of us can make with absolute certainty because our little brains can't process all there is to know about everything. At some point we have to choose to exercise faith—even in the shadow of doubt—and only time will determine if we made the right choice.

Wonder If...

Sometimes I've wondered what my life would have been like had I chosen to weave it with different threads. How would it have turned out? What would I have gained, and what would I have lost? Here are some of my musings:

- I probably would have made a lot more money, which would have been nice. I would have focused my skills with a relentless passion to achieve, regardless of the cost. I'm very determined and can do that. I'm sure I would have had a lot more toys and enjoyed playing with them.

- I'd probably have played a lot looser with the rules, creating my own truth that would've conveniently revolved around me and what I wanted. I'm sure my value of people would have been much lower, making it easier to hold grudges and write them off when they disagreed with me.

- I would have definitely been a charter member of the Schlitz Beer gang and grabbed for all the gusto I could. If this life is all there is, then there's not a minute to lose.

- I would have had way more ME time without the encumbrance of having to think so much about others, which can be exhausting. I definitely would have had a lot more free time on Sundays.

- I doubt my marriage would have lasted because that would have been stressful and limited my freedom to sample from the variety pack.

- I'm sure I would have done some things to help those in need, even if my heart wasn't in it, because that's what good people do. Not too much—just enough. Plus, I'd need the tax write-off.

Weaving my life with different threads would have definitely added some things to the plus side of the ledger—at least for a time. But then I've wondered if the benefits would have come at a cost that was more than I wanted to pay.

- Living by *my truth* would have invariably created conflicts that always grow in that kind of soil. My broken marriage would have brought pain to my family, and holidays with the kids and grandkids would have been a lot more complicated. I think the loneliness would have eventually caught up with me and I'd have found myself living with a whole lot of would've, could've, should've.

- My relentless quest for achievement would have undoubtedly left me with some deep regrets for the damage I'd caused others. My sleep probably wouldn't have been as restful for fear of incriminating secrets coming to light. And then, of course, there would've been the guilt.

- I'm sure…in time…I would have lost a sense of meaning and purpose because the thrill of money and achievement can only last so long. I think I'd have lived with a hole in my soul that was always asking, "Is this all there is?"

- I'm sure I would have lost the inner joy that comes from seeing how personal sacrifice can affect the lives of others in a way that makes you walk just a little taller.

- I would have lost the peace of mind and rest of soul that comes from knowing death is only a doorway to the best.

So, even if all the God threads I've woven into my life are just products of my imagination, I think I'd still have gone with them. They've given me a life of purpose, joy, peace, meaningful relationships, and few regrets. I like that. I'm choosing faith over doubt because, even in my darkness, the sun has always risen again. And I'm choosing faith in a loving God over faith in luck or coincidence because, while one gives me an inner sense of hope and value, the other leaves me cold and at the mercy of a great big lifeless nothing.

But There's More

Yet there's something far greater, something very personal and real that lives deep in my soul. It's something no human reasoning or logic-driven argument can take away. There is a day-to-day enjoyment of the love and presence of my heavenly Father—sometimes burning as a bright flame, sometimes only as a flicker—but always there, giving me a deep sense of peace and rest. The Apostle Paul described it like this:

> *The Spirit Himself testifies with our spirit that we are God's children.*
> Romans 8:16 NIV

I am a child of the living God and know it; I feel it, experience it, and love it. It's a reality that affects me at every turn, even with my doubts.

We talked earlier about the joy of crossing the finish line. Yet something I've noticed is that it's only those who are losing who want more time on the clock. Winners are always glad for the time to expire.

Some of you may feel like you're losing. While you've spent lots of time sedating your soul, you've never really experienced rest. All your convincing arguments against the invisible threads of God may have made you feel so *right*, but they've never given you the inner peace you long for.

At the close of the Apostle John's account of Jesus' life, he tells us the purpose of his writing:

> *...these have been written so that you may believe that Jesus is the Christ, the Son of God; and that by believing you may have life in His name.*
>
> John 20:30

He wrote this so you and I could experience the fulness of the life and love of Jesus.

If you find yourself unsure about Jesus, commit to reading John's gospel, starting at the beginning, for fifteen minutes every day for the next 30 days. Take weekends off if you'd like. Begin each day's reading by simply saying, "God, I don't even know if You're listening. But if You are, I'm asking You to show me You're real." Then begin reading and see what happens. If you run into something you don't understand, don't worry about it. Just move past it and keep going.

It's a small investment with the potential of a huge return. All of us are weaving threads into our lives that have to not only get us from here to the grave, but beyond. And eternity is a long time to be wrong.

For those of you who are followers of Jesus, my hope is that this book has given you a clearer understanding of God and yourself. The inner fabric of your life is created one stitch at a time, and if you're reading this, it means you're still in the game and have time to stitch. Choose your threads wisely because the story of your life depends on it.

God created each of us to live with a deep sense of peace and purpose as we navigate the chaos of our world. This can only happen as we overlay the unchanging reality of God on the ever-changing realities of our lives. It is the best gift we can give ourselves and those around us.

And when we do, we'll have stories to tell.

Come to Me, all who are weary and burdened, and I will give you rest. Take My yoke upon you and learn from Me, for I am gentle and humble in heart, and you will find rest for your souls. For My yoke is easy, and My burden is light.

JESUS

Postscript

MOVING FORWARD

I talked in the introduction about how disheartened I was at the seeming inability of too many followers of Jesus to live with a deep sense of peace and purpose in our ever-changing world. It is what motivated me to write my thoughts on the pages of this book, and my prayer is that it has helped you to sink your roots deeper into a fuller understanding of our wonderful God.

But we must always remember there is more. Athletes keep their bodies physically conditioned, not only to enjoy the benefits of good health but so they can engage in the arena of competition. In the same way, followers of Jesus keep their souls healthy, not only to experience peace in a world of chaos but so they can engage with God in His epic story of redemption. Living in the fullness of God means living with His heart for the world; picking up the baton and keeping the movement of Jesus advancing in our generation.

"Go therefore and make disciples of all the nations, baptizing them in the name of the Father and the Son and the Holy Spirit, teaching them to observe all that I commanded you; and lo, I am with you always, even to the end of the age."

Matthew 28:19-20

This can only happen when our souls are healthy and in love with the God who is in love with us. This is always the top priority.

But then it's time to move forward.

Therefore Project is a non-profit organization that was created to help envision, equip, and empower followers of Jesus to engage with Him as His official representatives in the world He loves.

*God reconciled us to Himself through Christ and gave us the ministry of reconciliation, namely, that God was in Christ reconciling the world to Himself, not counting their sins against them, and He has committed to us the word of reconciliation. **THEREFORE, we are ambassadors for Christ, as though God were making His appeal through us...***

2 Corinthians 5:18-20

Joining God in His redemptive movement means living as His ambassadors—official representatives— in helping others discover and step into a relationship with Him. While most growing followers of Jesus would love to be part of this, few ever are for two simple reasons:

- A feeling of inadequacy in being able to present the message of Jesus in a clear and under-standable way.

- The fear of being asked questions they don't know the answers to and feeling foolish.

This is not surprising since most are given little help to build their confidence as ambassadors. Normally all that's expected of them is to fund better church programming so they can invite their friends to join them. While this can be a good support, it's a poor substitute for what Jesus had in mind.

But help is on the way!

BiteSizeAnswers.com, an easy-to-use feature of **Therefore Project**, is designed to give you the support you need by providing:

- a quick, easy, and clear way to present the gospel of Jesus on a napkin, fast food bag, or anything you can sketch on.

- quick and easy answers to many complex questions, consisting of only two to three points that can be learned in just five minutes.

It's important to remember that those who are not followers of Jesus have questions, and they should. Never think of this as a threat but an opportunity. Every person at the core of their being longs to have a relationship with God, and we get the joy of working with Him as He draws people to Himself.

Some of you may be familiar with the field of apologetics, which is a defense of Christianity through the use of logical, historical, and scientific data. Many excellent books have been written on these subjects, and I've spent hundreds of hours absorbing the endless depths of knowledge and information.

Yet I've seldom used even a fraction of what I've learned to lead someone to faith in Christ. Sometimes it can even be a distraction because we get so focused on trying to prove a point that we never get to the life-changing message of Jesus. Usually, all that's needed is just enough information to *bump objections to the side* so you can communicate the good news:

> For I am not ashamed of the gospel, because **it is the power of God that brings salvation to everyone who believes...**
>
> Romans 1:16

We must never forget that it's the gospel alone—not proving the Bible's credibility or explaining why there's evil in the world—that has the power to reconcile people to God. While an understanding of apologetics can be helpful, one of its greatest values is building someone's confidence *after* they've come to faith in Christ.

The purpose of briefly answering questions is to give *just enough information* to clear the way for a simple presentation of the gospel. Just like the defense in a legal trial, the goal is not to prove innocence but to *create doubt*. Brief, thoughtful answers create just enough doubt so you can move to the gospel.

BiteSizeAnswers.com* is designed to do just that. When someone asks a question you're unsure of, you simply say, "That's a good question. Let me think about it for a few days and I'll get back with you." You then go to the website, click on your question, and find the answer in a five-minute video consisting of only two or three easy-to-remember points.

The goal is never to win arguments, but people

Therefore Project also provides both video and live training to equip and empower people to confidently live out and communicate the good news of Jesus.

Never forget that the key to everything is living with a healthy soul that is alive in the love and fullness of God. Weave the critical threads that make this possible into your life, then move forward into the great adventure of living as Ambassadors of Jesus in the world He loves.

For more information: info@ThereforeProject.com

*BiteSizeAnswers.com continues to grow each month. Check back if you don't find what you're looking for, or submit a question you'd like to have answered by visiting the website.

Footnote

As we saw earlier, everything has a life cycle that is bookended by a beginning and an end.

Therefore Project and Bite Size Answers are powerful and effective tools that have been created to envision, equip, and empower followers of Jesus to join Him as His official representatives in His redemptive story.

But someday these tools will have completed their life cycle and come to an end. So, if you're reading this book and can't find the websites, they may no longer exist.

But that doesn't change a thing! The gospel of Jesus Christ is still the power of God to transform the lives of those He loves, and He has still called each of us to join Him in His redemptive movement.

So avail yourself of effective tools and training that I know are out there to help you on your journey. Join with others who are doing the same, and keep your own soul alive and fresh in the wonder and fullness of God. He still loves the world, and still wants to communicate that love through you.

Acknowledgments

I remember having to write numerous papers in school, and the process was pretty straightforward. Pick a subject, create an outline, do the research, organize your findings into a logical presentation, and then make your case. It could be done in a matter of weeks, if not days.

But the writing of this book was nothing like that. It's taken a lifetime of learning and experience to bring my understandings to a logical presentation.

There's no question my life would have gone much differently without the profound influence of my parents. They modeled a commitment to God and others that, even though flawed, affected my thinking in ways that are still with me today. And if it hadn't been for the deep imprint of Herschel Martindale, made while sitting around a dining table in 1973, my choices could have gone in a very different direction. Both of these provided fertile soil for the seeds God was planting in my soul to grow.

I've been influenced over the years by hundreds of books and thousands of hours of teaching from gifted men and women. Many of these are reflected in the pages I've written, yet I don't know who to credit with what because, over time, their thoughts became mine. So if you've read something here that sounds like what others may have written or spoken, I say thank you to each of them. Their fingerprints are everywhere.

My many weeks of reflective solitude in mountain cabins over the years were made possible by the generosity of many cabin-owning friends: David and Carolyn Hill, Tim and Stephani Baker, Ron and Laura Sikes, and Sandy and Jane Shugart, just to name a few. The locations were so perfect that I've sometimes wondered if they kept them just for me.

The mechanics of taking ideas from concept to completion has required the help of so many. Thank you Greg Beardslee, Abbey Johnson, Austin Author, Jeff King, Jo Ann Forcino, and my wife for reading the early manuscripts and making valuable suggestions. Also, to Jack Levine, who not only read and critiqued the entire manuscript in just over a day, but helped to walk me through the maze of details involved in publishing.

Many of the things written here were developed, practiced, and taught during my years leading Fellowship Church in Texas and the Crossings Church in Florida. These wonderful people provided the healthy community of love, freedom, and support that is so necessary for learning to live the reality of God in uncharted waters. Thank you.

And finally, to all those who had to live around me— especially my wife, Joy—and endure the weirdness that comes from walking around with something always on your mind. You're the best!

About the Author

Ron Tewson spends his time helping people to integrate the reality of God into the reality of everyday life.

He tires of the same old answers and the same old practices that lead to the same old problems. He enjoys living in the freshness that comes from walking with God.

Born and educated in California, Ron spent his early years performing on stages throughout the United States and the world. The next four decades found him starting and running a successful business, planting and leading churches across the country, and speaking to thousands both nationally and internationally. Along the way he married, had five children, thirteen grandchildren, and a variety of dogs, cats, and other furry and feathered creatures. He lives with his wife, Joy, in Winter Garden, Florida.

Ron currently leads Therefore Project, writes, speaks, and talks with anyone who will listen about how knowing Jesus makes it possible to live every day in the peace, purpose, and love of God.

Therefore Project »»

You can connect with Ron at
RonTewson@ThereforeProject.com